THE JUDGMENT OF

KINGDOMS AND

NATIONS

A book to be kept in all families so that their children and their children's children may know the Birth-right, Liberty and Property of an Englishman

By the Chairman of the Committee commissioned to write the Bill of Rights 1688

John Somers

This book is about the rights, powers and governing prerogative of monarchs, as well as the rights, privileges and properties of the people.

Abridged and modernised for the contemporary reader.

By the people, for the people

To get in touch or request the full text of *The Judgement* in contemporary English script, email:
StandInHighamsPark@proton.me

Lord Somers was the author of the pamphlet *A Vindication of the proceedings of the late Parliament of England An. Dom. 1689, being the first in the reign of their present Majesties King William and Queen Mary* and served as Lord High Chancellor of England under King William III. He was also Chairman of the Committee responsible for drawing up the Declaration of Rights, which was published in the first act of William and Mary of Orange. The Declaration served as a foundation for the Bill of Rights 1688, which was drawn up by the same Committee and of which John Somers was likely the primary author. He bequeathed this little book to our nation and recommended *"**as proper to be kept in all Families, that their Children's Children may know the Birth-right, Liberty and Property belonging to an Englishman**"*.

We believe this to be the first contemporary edition of this historical pamphlet, based entirely on the text of the eleventh edition, originally published in 1714. We have taken the liberty of modernising, abridging and simplifying the text for the pleasure of the contemporary reader.

To honour the legacy of the bloodless revolution, which led to our current system of government and to spread this important message, **SITP Highams Park happily permits all readers to use, reproduce, circulate, transmit, store in retrieval systems, quote or otherwise use this publication, in whole or in part, as long as they refer to the source.**

Table of Contents

INTRODUCTION...1

    CREDIT TO LANCE PEATLING 3

    SNEAK PEEK:...4

PREFACE 5

THE CONTENTS 7

THE JUDGMENT OF KINGDOMS AND NATIONS 15

ANNEX I...99

    BILL OF RIGHTS [1688] 99

ANNEX II..109

    CORONATION OATH ACT 1688 109

ANNEX III...112

    ACT OF SETTLEMENT 1700 112

ANNEX IV...113

    THE CORONATION OATH OF CHARLES III (6 MAY 2023).......113

    THE OATH 113

The JUDGMENT of Whole Kingdoms and Nations, etc.

This book will show that **the nature of GOVERNMENT in general comes both from GOD and MAN**. This is an account of the British Government, and **the rights and privileges of the people** in the time of the Saxons, and since the Conquest.

It will show, by many examples in Scripture and history, that **all Magistrates and Governors proceed from the People, and their duties stem from Scripture and Reason**.

This is also an account of eleven emperors and more than fifty kings who were deprived of their thrones because of evil Government. **The people and parliament of Britain have the right to RESIST and REMOVE their Kings for evil Government**, by proof of King Henry's Charter of Liberties; many examples demonstrate that the same is true for Scotland.

The Prophets and the ancient Jews were strangers to absolute passive obedience. In most nations, resisting arbitrary government is allowed by many examples in Scripture, and by undeniable Reason.

This is a detailed account of the Glorious Revolution, including several speeches, declarations, and addresses, as well as the names and actions of ten bishops and over sixty peers, who actively participated in the Revolution before King James II left England.

Finally, this is an account of the several declarations in Queen *Elizabeth I's* time of the clergy in convocation and the parliament who assisted and

justified the resistance of the Scottish, French, and Dutch people against their evil and destructive princes.

1

The Eleventh Edition, corrected, and enter'd according to Law.

London. Printed and Sold by T. Harrison, at the West Corner of the Royal Exchange, in Cornhill, 1714. Price Stitch'd 6 *d.* and-Bound *1 Q d*

First Published in 1709 as "***Vox populi, vox dei***", being the true maxims of government

Lord John Somers, 1st Baron Somers

Credit to Lance Peatling

As luck would have it, after a long period of oblivion, this book was discovered by Lance Peatling at a time, when this great nation seemed to need its heritage the most. Lance quickly saw its value and announced it to all who would listen. After reading the facsimile edition, which was not an easy feat, he made a couple of videos and wrote an informative article. We recommend them to our precious readers and have provided the links below:

IMPORTANT INFO | Straight From The Horses Mouth - Lord Somers BOR 1688 Author

https://www.youtube.com/watch?v=UlXlZ5Hiybc

Lord Somers BOR 1688 - Lances Response To Comments! Just provide the evidence

https://www.youtube.com/watch?v=rmajMckKs5E&t=451s

Lance's article on substack:

https://lancepeatling.substack.com/p/standing-on-the-shoulders-of-giants

Sneak peek:

"Magna Carta is only a summary of our ancient laws and customs. The King that swears to it swears to them all."

"The King has no prerogative that derogates from justice and equality."

"The kings can neither make nor change laws. They are under the Law."

"The doctrine of absolute passive obedience is inconsistent with the goodness of God and the love he has for man. It destroys the purpose, intent and design of God's Laws, which are made to ensure man's happiness."

"Where there is no absolute authority, there can be no absolute obedience."

"He that lets any person destroy him contrary to law, when it is in his power to preserve his life by defending himself, tacitly consents to his own death. By the Laws of Nature, he is obliged to defend his life…"

Preface

Our little group, the Stand-In-The-Park (SITP) at Highams Park, took it upon ourselves to convert the old facsimile edition of this book to modern script for the benefit of all who want to remember and restore the natural order of society and life in England as it was re-established after the Glorious Revolution in 1688.

Lord John Somers was named as author in the 10th edition of this book. He was a man most active in laying the grounds for the revolution and chaired the Committee, which wrote both the Declaration of Rights and the Bill of Rights 1688.

To our knowledge, the 11th edition of 1714 was the last time this book was published back in the 1700s. This digest edition of 2024, which you now hold in your hands, appears to be the first since. We consider this book **an important legacy for the English people**. It was long lost but, thankfully, found in our hour of need. Now more than ever we need to be reminded that passive obedience to tyranny is unnatural, that the people are the principals of the governing power and that the people alone can choose to change their governors when the latter are no longer fit for purpose.

We use the opportunity to remind the reader that certain words, used in this book, evolved in meaning over time. For example:

Magistrate has its origin from the Latin words *magistratus*, which means "administrator" and *magister*, meaning "master" or "teacher". From the same origin comes the word *magnus* meaning "great". In Middle English, the meaning of ***magistrate*** tended to include a "judge or lawmaker", while today we mostly understand it to mean "justice of the peace" and/or a judge in the magistrate's court.

King has Germanic origin, *König*; it's related to the Dutch *koning* and to the Old English *cynn* meaning **"family, race"** (as in **kin**). Thus, the original meaning of **king** emerged as both a "relative, family member" and a "leader of people"; further, as illustrated by examples from natural history, it also means "a big dominant representative of a species" as in *king cobra*.

We remind the reader that the English society of the time was deeply religious and the Bible was studied as a matter of course, therefore, expect many biblical references. However, these are not there to indoctrinate but to prove an important point: **we are all created equal and when we chose to elevate a monarch to govern us, it is by consent which binds and restrains him. A king is only a king by law and, along with any man, is subject to the very law that makes him king. Most importantly, passive obedience to tyrannical power is the greatest crime and sin a man can commit**.

In addition, Latin was taught in all schools of renown at the time, hence, Latin phrases proliferate in this text, which were then in popular use in the circles of educated men. We have minimised their number and provided translations to the best of our capacity.

§

THE CONTENTS

¶ Paragraphs 1 to 6. The Nature of Government in General both from God and Man.

¶ 6. An Account of the British Government, and of the Rights and Privileges of the People, in the Time of the Saxons, and since the Conquest.

¶ 7. There is no natural rule for choosing Government.

¶ Paragraphs 8 to 17 and paragraphs 19, 21 to 38. True Maxims of Government.

¶ 18. The Power of the Crown is only a Trust.

¶ 20. Britain is a mixed limited monarchy.

¶ Paragraphs 28 to 35. Absolute monarchy is inconsistent with civil society.

¶ 39 to 46. Historical account of Government ordained by God over the Children of Israel.

¶ 46, 47. The fundamental right of all nations to choose their governors and forms of government.

¶ 48. Description of the Liberty and Customs of the Ancient Britons.

¶ 49. Monsieur Mezeray's account of the manners of the ancient Germans[1].

---

[1] Reference to the French historian François Eudes de Mézeray (1610-1683).

¶ 50. 51, 52. The election of Magistrates and Kings is proved to be in the People, particularly in Great Britain, before and since the Conquest.

¶ 53. The Right of the People and Parliament of Britain to resist and depose their Kings for Evil Government; proved from King *Henry*'s Charter of Liberties and by many Examples.

¶ 54, 55, 56. The Power of our Parliaments.

¶ 57. By a Law, Anno[2] 787 Kings were to be elected by the Parliament or States.

¶ 58. William I was admitted by the People, upon conditions.

¶ 59, 60. The Law superior to the King, from Bracton, a famous Lawyer in Henry III's Reign.

¶ 61. The Power of the King, by the Laws of Edward the Confessor.

¶ 62. William Rufus, Henry V, and Stephen were chosen by the People; and Henry IV, V and VI were Kings (only) by Act of Parliament.

¶ 63, 64. The Compact[3] with William, called *the* Conqueror, Henry V, and Stephen.

¶ 65. The Original Compact with our Kings (Magna Carta).

¶ 66, 67, 68. Succession gives no Right to Kings, except according to the Original Compact. Magna Carta is only an Abridgement of our ancient Laws and Customs.

¶ 69,70,71. The Nobility and Parliament of England assert the Laws and Liberties of England.

¶ 72. King James's Speech in 1609.

---

[2] From Latin meaning "year"
[3] Archaic meaning "contract"

¶ 73, 74. The common Right of the Subject, declared by several ancient Lawyers.

¶ 75, 76, 78, 79 Our Kings and their Power from the Laws, declared by several famous Lawyers and by several Acts of Parliament.

¶ 77. Six Judges, including one of the King's Council at Law, were condemned by Parliament, and executed for giving their Opinions contrary to Law, in Richard II's Time.

¶ 80. King Henry the VIII acknowledged the Power of the Parliament.

¶ 81. The Judges of the Land should not obey the King if his command is contrary to Law, under the Penalty of Treason.

¶ 82. The Rights and Liberties of the Subject from the Act of William and Mary, with a Clause excluding a Popish Prince or any marrying a Papist from the Throne.

¶ 83, 84. All Government, Authority, and Magistracy proceeds from the People, and they have Authority to dispossess them or alter the Succession.

¶ 85, to 100. More than fifty Kings, and eleven Emperors were deprived for their Evil Government in France, Spain, Holland, Portugal, Denmark, Poland, Rome, Germany, Scotland, and England.

¶ Paragraphs 101 to 107 and ¶ 111. All Magistrates and Governors proceed from the People, by many examples in Scripture. The Duty of all Magistrates, from Scripture and Reason.

¶ 108, 109, 110. Reasons for Resistance.

¶ 112. Description of Just Government and of Obedience to the Laws.

¶ 113. Neither Absolute Authority, nor Absolute Obedience is allowed.

¶ 114. The Laws were made by the People in the Reign of Darius[4].

¶ 115, to 122. Reasons against absolute passive obedience.

¶ 123 to 125. The bishops defend King James and refuse to sign an Abhorrence of the Prince of Orange's intended Invasion.

¶ 126. The Prince of Orange's Speech to the Gentry of Somersetshire and Dorsetshire.

¶ Paragraphs 127 to 129. Massive support for the Prince of Orange.

¶ 130. The Address of the Lieutenancy of London to the Prince, Dec. 11, 1688.

¶ 131. The Lord Mayor, Aldermen, and Common Council's Address to the Prince.

¶ 132. The Names of ten of the Privy-Council and Peers who made an Order on the 14th of Dec. 1688 for all Irish Soldiers to deliver up their Arms.

¶ 133, 134. Welcoming the Prince of Orange. The Speech of Sir George Treby, Recorder of London, to the Prince, Dec. 20, 1688.

¶ 135 to 149. About sixty Peers sign an Association to the Prince. Fifty-four Lords Spiritual and Temporal made an Order for Squire Gwinn to sign such Orders as they should, from time to time. The Address of the aforesaid Peers to the Prince of Orange.

¶ 140, 141. The Convention ordered a Day of Thanksgiving for the great Deliverance. On the 28th of January the Commons voted the Throne vacant and on the 6th of February the Lords consented to the said Vote.

¶ 142. The Word "abdicated" explained.

---

[4] King Darius the Great (c. 550-486 BCE), the third Persian King of the Achaemenid Empire. The Persian Empire reached its peak during his reign.

¶ 143, 144. The Prince and Princess of Orange proclaimed King and Queen.

¶ 145. The Declaration of the Nobility, Gentry and Commonalty at Nottingham.

¶ 146. Our Bishops, Clergy, Nobility, etc. are damned, who kept with the Doctrine of absolute passive obedience.

¶ 147. The Doctrine of *Jure Divino* never heard of until James I's Reign.

¶ 148. No absolute passive obedience in the time of the Children of Israel, proved by many examples of their resisting their Kings.

¶ 149. The Primitive Christians, among others, resist their Emperors for their Tyranny.

¶ Paragraphs 150 to 153. Several Declarations in Queen Elizabeth's time and defence of the Protestants in their resisting of their Evil Princes and giving money to assist the Scottish, French, and Dutch Protestants.

¶ 154. The Protestant Princes of Germany resist their Emperors.

¶ Paragraphs 155 to 160. Bishops in defence of Resistance. Seven Princes and twenty-four protestant cities resist their Emperor.

¶ 162, 163, 164, Zwingli[5], one of the first Reformers, Lucifer de Cagliari[6], St. Athanasius[7] and St. Austin[8] for Resistance.

---

[5] Ulrich Zwingli (1484-1531) was a leader of the Reformation in Switzerland.

[6] Lucifer was a bishop of Cagliari in Sardinia in the 4th century. He was known for his passionate opposition to Arianism (i.e. denying the divinity of Christ).

[7] Athanasius I of Alexandria (died 373 AD) was the 20th patriarch of Alexandria. He was a famous defender of Christian Orthodoxy.

[8] Also known as St Augustine of Hippo (354-430 AD). Skilled preacher and rhetorician, he was one of the Latin Fathers of the Church and was formally recognised as Doctor of the Church.

¶ 165. The successful Resistance in several countries.

¶ 166. The Difference between our case and that of the first primitive Christians.

¶ 167, 168. The Prophets and ancient Jews, as well at the primitive Christians, were strangers to the Doctrine of absolute passive obedience.

¶ 169. Absolute Obedience is due only to our Laws.

¶ 170, 171. Just Resistance is founded in self-defence and absolute submission is self-murder.

¶ Paragraphs 172 to 179. Several reasons against the passive obedience doctrine.

¶ 181 to 183. The Patriarchal scheme considered and refuted.

¶ 184. An objection answered (if Government be disturbed by unlawful proceedings, how can it be safe).

¶ 185. Rulers or Subjects, overturning the Constitution is the greatest crime of all.

¶ 186, 187, 188. An Account of the Government of King Charles I, taken out of Lord Clarendon's History[9], Rushworth's Collection[10] and Whitlock's Memorials[11] without any observation or reflection.

---

[9] *The History of the Rebellion and Civil Wars in England* by Edward Hyde, 1st Earl of Clarendon, originally written between 1646 and 1648.

[10] John Rushworth (c. 1612 – 12 May 1690) was an English lawyer, historian and politician who sat in the House of Commons at various times between 1657 and 1685. He compiled a series of works covering the English Civil Wars throughout the 17th century called Historical Collections and also known as the Rushworth Papers.

[11] An account of the events in Europe between 1660 and 1680.

¶ 189. Dr. Sacheverell's assertion that the Prince of Orange disclaimed all Resistance, disproved from the 25th Paragraph of his Declaration.

<u>ANNEXES</u> (offered for convenience and expediency)

Annex I: **The Bill of Rights 1688**

Annex II: **The Coronation Oath Act 1688**

Annex III: **Part IV of the Act of Settlement 1700** (the people's birth right)

Source for all of the above Annexes:
https://www.legislation.gov.uk/

Annex IV: **The Coronation Oath of Charles III as administered on 6 May 2023**

Source:
https://www.royal.uk/sites/default/files/documents/2023-05/23-24132%20Coronation%20Liturgy_05%20May_0.pdf

JOHN SOMERS

THE JUDGMENT OF KINGDOMS AND NATIONS

¶ **1. Government in general**, as intended and instituted by God, **is constrained by the laws of nature and service to the benefit of mankind**. All rulers are confined by the Almighty Supreme Sovereign to exert their governing power for the promotion of God's dominion and to **exercise their authority for the safety, welfare, and prosperity of those over whom they are established**. Although there were no previous contracts and agreements between princes and people, the princes are obliged to observe these rules, since they are determined by the Divine Legislator and Universal Sovereign.

Therefore, if anyone refuses to govern in subservience to God and in protection and benefit of the community, he ceases to fulfil the goals for which magistracy[12] was instituted.

It is the choice and power of any society to set up the forms of government, under which they are contented to live, and nominate the persons to whom they confer the right to administer justice. It is not, however, their choice to extend the powers of those whom they

---

[12] At the time, *magistracy* was associated much more with administering the affairs of the state than with judging or dispute resolution. Today a *magistrate* means mostly "justice of the peace" in a Magistrate's Court.

constitute their rulers[13] beyond the limits and boundaries by which God has confined magistrates in the Charter of Nature and Revelation[14].

People may at any time restrict themselves as they choose in matters under their own disposal to either decrease or increase the ruler's power, in reference to what they can retain or depart from, for the real or imagined benefit of the community. Yet they can in no way intervene in the rights granted by God[15], which He has reserved to Himself; nor can they confer such degrees of authority upon elected magistrates, which God has already prohibited the one from granting and the other from receiving.

For example, **no body or society of men can _transfer a power_ to those selected from among themselves to govern the community, which would allow those with delegated magisterial authority to withdraw their subjects from their allegiance to God, or act arbitrarily in imposing any religion, or destroy the meanest person, saving upon a previous crime and a just demerit.**

¶ **2.** No man of common sense can imagine that governments existed at the first propagation of mankind. But in those times each father, without being subject to any superior power, governed his wife, children, and servants.

It seems very probable that even at the time of the Deluge, there was no magistracy or civil constructs, but that all government was lodged only in each father of a family.

---

[13] Etymologically, the word "rule" stems from the Latin _regula_ (straight stick) and _regulare_ (to straighten or keep straight). In Middle English its meaning was associated with directing and governing, not with dictating or commanding.

[14] Reference to St Paul who believed the Book of Nature was the source of God's revelation to humankind. Not to be confused with the UN World Charter for Nature 1982.

[15] The rights granted by God are referred to as unalienable rights, for example the right to live, the right to shelter from the environment, the right to breathe clean air, the right to clean water, the right to self-defence, etc.

It is hard to imagine that the exercise of laws and magistracy would lead to such abominable disasters. It is easy to see that once the rules of government were established, mankind did not face any calamities causing the purging of the world.

¶ **3.** In the institution of magistracy, God has confined those chosen as rulers to govern for the good of those over whom they came to be established. **It remains entirely up to the people at their first election of government to define the measures and boundaries of the public good, as well as to what rules and standards the magistrate must be bound to defend and promote the benefit of the society** to which he is endorsed as a civil and political Head.

Everyone is equally master of his own property and liberty, subject to their prior agreement with one another, and to the Compact of the Universality[16]. **It evidently follows that those who come to be clothed with magistracy can claim no more liberty or right over the property of that Body Politic[17] than that which the community has conferred upon them.**

We must assume all mankind to have gone mad if they should submit themselves to the jurisdiction of one who had no original right to command them and/or if they end up in a worse condition than they were previously. And therefore, seeing that the extent of the magistrate's power must originate from a grant of the People, it is incumbent upon the magistrate to prove and justify their authority and privilege.

---

[16] The Compact of the Universality pertains to the social contract between those governing and those accepting governance, where universality in particular relates to all natural rights belonging to all people.

[17] *Body politic* historically means a city or state, metaphorically considered as a physical body. The monarch was typically depicted as the head, while the analogy might be extended to other anatomical parts as in Aesop's fable "The Belly and Members".

And what he cannot derive from a concession of the society must be acknowledged to remain still vested in the People as their reserved privilege and right. Whatever adverse power he exercises over them, which he cannot prove has been surrendered to him, demonstrates a breach of his contract with the community.

As he was ordained ruler by virtue of that contract, this renders him guilty of an invasion upon the rights of the whole society and upon every individual member of it. Force or conquest give no just or legal title over a people until the people declare their acquiescence to him by consent upon the best terms which they can obtain, and he is willing to grant.

No civil government is lawful unless founded on contract and agreement between those chosen to govern and those who accepted to be governed. The articles upon which they first stipulated the one with the other become the fundamentals of the respective constitutions of nations and together with added positive laws, are both the limits of the ruler's authority and the measures of the subject's obedience.

To extend the governor's right to command and the subject's duty to obey beyond the laws of one's country is treason against the constitution and betrayal to society. Every prince is tempted to dissolve the ties by which he stands confined and overthrow the fences protecting the reserved rights, privileges and properties of the subjects. This is how a prince becomes a tyrant and makes all his subjects slaves. **All previous agreements and laws are made insignificant by the evil doctrine of *non-resistance* when our rights are arbitrarily invaded, and the Constitution openly attacked.** Such a doctrine tricks and cheats those who were originally free into a state of bondage.

¶ 4. As it is by virtue of contracts and agreements, all legal governments are established by various and distinct forms in different countries. The title and right to exercise authority and the method of arriving at it is provided for so that **every subject's allegiance is owing first to the Constitution and only then to the ruler, and only to the extent of the binding terms of the original pact.** Outside the constitution and the obligations it creates for us, no man can presume a right to command us, nor do we owe him any duty of obedience.

If anyone does subvert the fundamental laws of the society under a pretence of being constituted sovereign, he thereby, *ipso facto*[18], **annuls his legal right to govern and absolves all who were previously his subject, from the legal obligations to yield him obedience.** Thus, the immediate and natural effect of a prince claiming more than what the rules of the constitution entitle him to prevents him from it and deprives him of all right to claim anything. It restores the people to their state of primitive freedom, of which they only divested themselves upon **the terms of the constitution, which should be kept sacred and inviolable.**

So, it follows from the above-mentioned contracts **that one person is advanced from the common level to the authority of a Sovereign and that all others are, by their own consent, put into the condition of subjects.** A mutual relationship arises between the one who governs and those who are governed, but **the first and highest treason is that which is committed against the Constitution.** Any crimes against the person of the supreme Magistrate are only declared to be so to ensure his defence of the Constitution and because, to protect the peace, welfare, and safety of society, he should be protected from danger and rendered sacred in his person and inviolable in his regal honour. He must not depart from the fundamental terms of the original contract, nor from provisions added and enacted afterwards to preserve the government in its rudimentary state.

Those who endeavour to preserve and maintain the Constitution can never be traitors; the traitors are those who pursue the subversion of it. The first and highest treason is when a member of the political society acts to subvert the Constitution. Yet it is also the greatest treason to act against the person, crown, and dignity of the King as such actions would invalidate his superiority over the rest of the people who granted it to him **by virtue of the Constitution.** He would be deprived of all rightful and legal claim to govern the society if he acts to destroy

---

[18] Latin: by the fact itself, because of that fact

its foundation. Acting in violation of the Charter, from which he derives and holds his governing power, makes his title to sovereignty precarious and renders every claim of governing the community to be an invasion and usurpation.

¶ **5.** I will only add that as **all legal government is founded upon a mutual stipulation and contract, the first and most absolute obligation arising from it lies with the Prince towards the People; yet their fealty and duty to him, binding though it is under that contract, is but secondary and conditional.**

Whenever any person is chosen from the rest of society and raised to kingship based on a prior contract with the community, he becomes, upon the very accepting it, bound absolutely and without reserve to govern the people according to the terms agreed and stipulated, and to rule them by the Laws to which they have confined him. **Those who have rendered themselves subjects under that agreement owe their created Sovereign all due obedience and fealty but only if he governs them in accordance with the agreed terms and protects their privileges, liberties and rights.**

¶ **6.** Great Britain has been the most provident of all countries in reserving to itself, upon the first institution of regal government, all such rights, privileges, and liberties as were necessary to make it renowned abroad as well as safe, happy, and prosperous at home. With courage and magnanimity, it has maintained its privileges and liberties through the ages and has secured them by new and superadded laws whenever there were endeavours to undermine and supplant them. Further, it has vindicated its Constitution even to the extent of depositing treacherous, usurping, and tyrannical princes when more gentle, lawful methods were found ineffectual.

The people of Britain have the same title to the enjoyment of their liberties and properties that our kings have to their crown and regal dignity. As kings, they can only claim to endorse fundamental and positive Laws, therefore, the subjects' interest in their liberty and property is conveyed by the same terms and channels and protected with the same hedges.

Horn tells us in his Mirror[19], *That the Saxons having put an End to the Heptarchy, [...]* **they chose themselves one King to maintain and defend their Persons and Goods in Peace, by Rules of Law, and made him swear, that he should be obedient to suffer Right as well as his People should be.**

According to Bracton[20], *The Whole Power of the King of* England, *is to do Good, and not to do Hurt; nor can he do any thing as a King, but what he can legally do.*

Hence, our Princes were and are bound to swear at their Coronation that *they would govern according to Law, and preserve unto them all their Customs, and Franchises* (Stat of Provis. 25.)

It is worth noting what Henry I wrote to the Pope, when attacked by him about the matter of investitures, viz. *That he could not diminish the Rights either of the Crown or of the Kingdom, and that if he should be so abject and mean as to attempt it, the Barons and People of England represented in Parliament, would not allow or permit it.* Thus, it is affirmed of an English King, "**that he can do no Wrong, because he can do nothing but what the Law empowers him**".

As **King, he has all things subjected to his authority while he acts according to law, yet there is nothing left to his arbitrary will.** The several Charters, especially the one titled *The Great Charter*, in and by which our rights are secured to us and to our posterity, were not the grants and concessions of our princes, but recognitions of what we have

---

[19] Andrew Horn, author of *Mirroir des Justices* (Mirror of Justice) who served as Chamberlain of the city of London between 1320 and 1328, the year of his death, was considered "one of the most learned lawyers of his day", as described in William Blacksone's *Commentaries on the Laws of England*

[20] Henry de Bracton (c. 1210-1268) became famous with his writings on law, in particular *De legibus et consuetudinibus Angliæ* ("On the Laws and Customs of England")

reserved unto ourselves in the original establishment of our government, and of what had always belonged to us by common law and immemorial customs.

Although these privileges and liberties came to be more distinctly expressed and unmistakably ratified in the Great Charter, they had been acknowledged and passed down in the Laws of Edward the Confessor as the **Birthright of every Englishman**. Prior to that, William, the first Norman King, also ratified them. Yet long before that King Edgar the Saxon had collected them in a book, which the Confessor only revised, repeated, and confirmed.

Among all the rights and privileges belonging to us, that of having a share in the legislation and being governed by such laws as we ourselves may choose is the most fundamental and essential, as well as the most advantageous and beneficial. For thereby we are enabled to make successive and continual provisions for the preservation of society and the promotion of the temporal and eternal welfare of the subject. By our possession of so great a portion of the legislative power and by our right to annual parliaments, **we can act against any threat, danger, or oppression, and we can provide the whole community with all legal aids and means necessary for peace, preservation, and prosperity**. So, herein lies our signal advantage and felicity that **what we become interested in becomes, then and there, a part of our right and property by a positive statute law and is not to be taken from us but by our own consent**.

As Bracton said, though it is also one of the first dictates of reason and common sense, **Laws can neither be altered nor vacated, save by the consent and concurrence of the same authority by which they were made and enacted. It is true that the executive part of the government is, both by our common and statute laws, conveyed to and vested in the King. At the same time, there is sufficient provision made in the terms of our constitution and in our parliamentary Acts to prevent this from hurting us,** unless our sovereigns become guilty of the highest treachery and endeavour the subversion of the whole government.

The right of overseeing the execution of the laws is a prerogative inseparable from the office of the supreme magistrate, because the very ends to which he is given governing authority and for which he is designed and established are the conservation of the public peace and the administration of justice towards and among the members of the body politic.

The wisdom of our ancestors, as practiced by them upon the first institution of civil government, was to direct, limit, and restrain the executive power conferred onto the Sovereign, and to make him and his subordinate ministers accountable in case they deny, delay or pervert justice, or are charged with maladministration of the laws.

Our predecessors and ancestors have been exceptionally foresighted for they have left nothing to the king's private discretion, much less to his arbitrary will, but have assigned him the laws as the rules and measures to govern by. They not only delegated it to him as a trust, which he was to swear faithfully to perform, but they have always reserved a liberty, right, and power for themselves to inspect his administration, making him responsible for it. This right and power could also abdicate him from the sovereignty if he were to commit egregious failures in the trust credited and consigned to him. Of this we have indisputable evidence in the articles advanced in parliament against Richard II when he was deposed from the throne and had the sceptre taken out of his hand.

To prevent any dangers which might befall us because of our trusting the king with the executive power of government, our constitution and laws provide that he is not allowed to do anything in his own person. Not so much as to draw and seal the commission of those that are to act in his name and under him, as in our government nothing is considered a commission, but what the law authorizes and warrants.

Acting under the imaginary authority of an illegal commission is a greater crime than it would be to commit the same crime without any colour and pretence of power or warrant. The former affects all: the king, the government, and the whole body of the people. To reinforce and secure us from abuse of the executive power lodged in the king, all of the king's commissions must be legal or else considered null and void. Even those warranted and empowered by legal commissions are to be sworn to execute them legally or be punished for everything they do upon them that deviates from the measures of the law.

It has been the duty and practice of just and honourable princes, who have been faithful to the trust vested in them, to punish their officers and ministers for corruption and for departing in their administration from the rules of our common and statute laws. King Alfred caused forty-four justices to be hanged in one year for illegal, false, and corrupt Judgments. So, it is up to our parliaments to enquire into and punish the crimes of judges and all others employed by and under the king in the executive part of the government, as this is one of the reasons for which they ought to be frequently called and assembled.

Thus, **by the constitution**, among other capacities in which they fit and act, **the House of Commons are to be the great inquest of the kingdom and investigate all oppressions and injustices of the king's ministers**. Likewise, among their several other rights and privileges, **the House of Lords stand clothed with the power and authority of the High Court of Judicature of the nation**, empowered to punish any who have misbehaved themselves in the courts, as well as those wrongfully justified by conniving inferior courts. Of this all ages afford us precedents and our ancestors used to make frequent examples of parliamentary justice among our late kings' ministers and officers forgoing our laws. The only reason we have had so many usurpations and incursions of the laws, immunities, rights, and privileges of the nation is because we have neglected all such precedents.

¶ 7. **There is no natural or divine law for any form of government**. No natural rule exists for choosing one person rather than another to administer foreign affairs or have power over other families, who are all equal by nature, being of the same rank and born to the same use of the same common faculties. Therefore, **all of mankind is at liberty to choose the form of government they like best**.

Does anyone believe that God was not as much concerned for Italy when it had but one prince, as now when it has so many? The same with

Germany and Switzerland, which was once one commonwealth under the dukes and marquises, but was then divided into cantons under popular magistrates of their own? England was first a monarchy under the Britons and then a province under the Romans, and after that divided into seven kingdoms at once under the Saxons, and after them the Danes, and then the Normans, and now a monarchy again under the English, and all this by God's providence.

God approves of such magistrates that the community thinks fit to appoint. This is plain by the testimony of the Holy Scripture when God said to Solomon, *By me Kings rule, and Nobles, even all the Judges of the Earth*, Proverbs 8. 16. That is, they govern by his permission, though chosen by the people.

¶ **8. All political societies began from a voluntary union and mutual agreement of men** freely acting in the choice of their governors and forms of government.

¶ **9. The safety of the people is the supreme law and what the people have enacted by common consent and for the public safety they may change when things require it, by the same common consent.**

¶ **10.** The rightful power of making laws to command whole societies of men properly belongs to those same entire societies. If any prince were to exercise it by himself and not by express authority as initially derived from their consent, it would be tyranny. ***Laws they are not which public approbation has not made so***. Hooker's Eccl.[21].

---

[21] Richard Hooker, author of "Of the Lawes of Ecclesiasticall Politie" (1593–97), reconciling Thomist doctrines of transcendent and natural law.

¶ **11.** Aristotle says: *Whoever is governed by a man without laws, is governed by a man and a beast.*

¶ **12.** Aristotle also said, "*The whole Kingdom, City or Family is more excellent and to be preferred before any part or member thereof.*"

¶ **13.** By the laws of nature, the welfare of the people is both the supreme and first law in government, and the scope and end of all other laws.

¶ **14. No human law is binding which is contrary to Scripture, or the general laws of Nature.**

¶ **15. Religion does not overthrow nature, whose chief principle is to preserve herself.**

¶ **16.** As magistrates were designed for the public good, so must the obligation to them be understood to be for the same main purpose: **the reason of all law and government is the public good**.

¶ **17.** A just governor acting for the benefit of the people cares more of the public good and welfare than of his own private advantage.

¶ **18. The power that is lodged in the crown is only a trust and nothing more, for no prince has any right to the throne other than what the laws of the land or the voice of the people give him.** Before he is a magistrate, a man cannot have a right by nature, nor more power or authority from God, than another man. All men have power from God to do either good or evil, and God Almighty permits them to do either. The prince has his authority from the people or the law, which chooses or appoints him to be supreme, of which he is only executor. **The law is the only rule and power of his government** (and the measure of the people's obedience), beyond which he has no just or rightful power in his political capacity.

¶ **19.** **The supreme authority of a nation belongs to those who have the ultimate legislative authority. It does not belong solely to the executive, which is plainly a trust when separated from the legislative power. All trusts, by their nature, purport that those to whom trust is given are accountable, even though no such condition is expressly specified.**

¶ **20.** All who know anything of Britain know that its government is a mixed limited monarchy, where the supreme power is divided between the King and the People (i. e. the Lords and Commons). Without them the king can neither raise money, nor make or annul laws and those laws are a rule to both. **The laws are a common measure, to him of his power and to them of their obedience.** The government is called a monarchy because, under the Constitution, the king has a share in the supreme power and the chief executive administration is singly with him.

¶ **21.** In every government there must be in a power to preserve itself not only against force from *without*, but against violence and destruction from *within*, just like a man preserves his body from diseases and defends it against violence. A man cannot renounce this power, because **self-preservation is and always will be a duty**. Likewise, neither can a people united in society or government renounce the power of maintaining that society or government. The instrument of their safety and preservation is **the condition that all subjects are equal, whether under absolute or limited government**. If it were not lawful to maintain and preserve those limitations, the king's will and pleasure, and not the law, would be the measure of obedience, **for to have liberties and privileges, which may not be defended, is to have none at all**.

¶ **22.** **Laws and Oaths in limited governments are ties upon the King and People must serve as fences for the constitution and not as handles to overthrow it. The Coronation Oath and the Oath of Allegiance are, in effect, swearing to the Constitution, one to govern and the other to be governed in accordance with it.**

However, if a Coronation Oath is a king's tie only to God and the Oath of Allegiance is extended to absolute subjection, then both King and People swear against the Constitution instead of to maintain it, as they ought to do.

¶ **23.** The laws are the nerves and sinews of societies and, as the magistrate is above the people in his legal capacity, **so is the law above the magistrate, or else there could be no safety to the Constitution**.

¶ **24.** **He who makes himself above all law is no member of a commonwealth, but a tyrant.**

¶ **25.** He who destroys another has quitted the rule of justice and equity between men and has put himself into a state of war with the other.

¶ **26.** **No man in civil society can be exempted from the laws of it**. There must be redress or security against the greatest mischief the prince may do or cause to be done by others, so that every man in that society is in a state of nature[22] with respect to all.

¶ **27.** The principles of natural religion give those in authority no power at all, but only secures them in the possession of that which is theirs by the laws of the country.

¶ **28. Absolute monarchy is inconsistent with civil society** and can, therefore, be no form of civil government.

¶ **29.** No man or society of men has power to deliver up their preservation or the means of it to the absolute will of any man. **Men will always have the right to preserve what they have no power to part with.**

¶ **30.** No power can exempt princes from the obligation to the eternal laws of God and Nature. **In all disputes between power and liberty, power must always be proved, but liberty proves itself**, with the one being founded upon positive law and the other upon the laws of nature.

¶ **31.** If a magistrate, notwithstanding all good laws made for the governing of a community, will act destructively to that community, **the people are discharged from both active and passive obedience, and become indispensably obliged by the law of nature to resist.**

---

[22] Reference to John Locke's belief that the state of nature was a peaceful existence where all men are independent and equal yet respect the laws of nature equally.

¶ **32.** If a man be a wolf to man, any man would will it to be a God to men. Antiquity has enrolled Hercules amongst the number of the Gods because he punished the tyrants, the pests of mankind, and the monsters of the world.

¶ **33. The same reason that obliges the people to obey governors and magistrates, when they govern according to the laws and Constitution of the country and act for the good of society, does as much oblige the people to oppose them if they design the people's ruin or destruction.** How can God, who commands mankind to preserve their lives and use any means necessary to that end, require that people suffer their own destruction or be made slaves to gratify the brutishness of any one man, or a few who are by nature their equals but only above them by serving in an office, established by the people for their own convenience?

¶ **34.** When the Christian religion has become a part of the subject's property by the laws and Constitution of the country, then it is to be considered as one of their principal rights and may be defended as any other civil right.

¶ **35. A cause is just if it defends the laws, protects the common good, and preserves the state.** A cause is unjust if it violates the laws, defends the lawbreakers, and protects the subverters of the Constitution. That is just which destroys tyrannical government. That is unjust which would abolish a just government.

¶ **36.** What can be more absurd than to say, "*There is an absolute subjection due to a Prince if the Laws of God, Nature, and the Country have not given him Authority?*" Men who say so are herds of cattle or beasts of burden, made for the prince's use.

¶ **37.** The reign of a good king resembles that of heaven, over which there is but one God, for he is no less beloved of the virtuous than feared of the bad.

¶ **38.** It is not the title of a king, but the power derived from the laws with which he is vested, that makes the difference between him and other men. His person is sacred and, whilst he continues to be the king, not to be resisted. He is above each member of society and, therefore, cannot be deprived of his office unless he turns into an enemy of his kingdom.

¶ **39.** The government which God ordained over the children of Israel consisted of three parts, besides the magistrates of the several tribes and cities. They had a chief magistrate, who was called judge or captain, such as Joshua, Gideon, and others; a council of 70 chosen men; and the general assemblies of the people. These judges or captains had not the name or power of kings, nor was their power transmitted to their children, but granted occasionally as required.

When the tribes of Reuben, Gad, and half of Manasseh had built an altar by Jordan, the whole congregation of Israel gathered at Shiloh to go to war against them and sent Phineas the priest and ten princes of the congregation with a message.

And the like assembly Joshua called to Shechem composed of all the people or tribes of Israel, and he called for their elders, their heads of families, their judges and other officers, and Joshua spoke to all the people. They agreed with him, and he made a Covenant and Law with them before the Lord, which was written in the *Book of the Law, Joshua 24.*

¶ **40.**

After Joshua's death, every tribe acted on the decisions made at their own assemblies.

¶ 41.

When the sons of Samuel were judges over Israel, they took bribes and perverted justice, so the elders of Israel asked Samuel to choose them a king. There were delegates from the whole congregation and God said to Samuel, *"**Hearken to the Voice of the People in all that they say unto thee**"*, I Samuel VIII 4, 7.

The Jews, in their creating of judges, kings or other magistrates, had no regard to paternity. God never directed them to do it, nor rebuked them for neglecting it. If they would choose a king, he commanded them to choose one of their brethren by lot, and caused the lot to fall upon Saul, a young man of the youngest tribe. David and the other kings of Israel and Judaea had no more to say for themselves in that point than Saul.

All the kings of that nation were raised, justly or unjustly, with no regard to any prerogative they could claim or appropriate. All that they had, therefore, was from the people who elevated them. It was impossible for the people to give power to kings if they did not have it themselves. This power, which we call liberty, universally resides in everyone. When God gave liberty to His people to make a king, He neither constituted nor elected any until the people desired it. God did not command them to have a king but left it to their own free will to decide whether they would have a king or not.

Every Israelite could have been chosen; none but strangers were excluded. The people were left to the liberty of electing any one of their brethren. But the whole history of the Jews shows that the pride, magnificence, pomp, and glory usurped by their kings was utterly contrary to the will of God. They did lift their hearts above their brethren, which was forbidden by the Law of God.

¶ **42.** Josephus[23] says, *They may do nothing without the advice of the Sanhedrin or if they do, it shall be opposed.* This agrees with the Confession of Zedekiah to the princes: *"The King can do nothing without you"*, Jeremiah XXXVIII. This was pursuant to the Law of that kingdom, which was written in a book and laid up before the Lord. They were not to govern by their own will, but according to the law from which they might not recede. **This was the Law of God, not to be abrogated by man; a law of liberty, directly opposite to submitting to the will of any one man.**

¶ **43.** The manner of the kingdom signified the constitution of the government, which meant the conditions on which Saul was to be king and the people his subjects. **Although God had given him the crown, it was to rule the people according to justice and laws, which meant frequently *going in and out before them*, referring to justice being executed in times of peace and war.** The king was to lead them in *one*, and direct in the *other*. This manner of the kingdom was told to all the people. It implied the consent of the people was required to make him king. The contract between Saul and the people, *being written in a book and laid before the Lord*, was a very good equivalent to an Oath, recorded on both sides as an Oath of Allegiance and an Oath of Government.

They desisted him and said, *"How shall this man save us?"*, Samuel X 27. They saw no merit in the young man. The king they expected should have been a man of tried and tested conduct, valour, and bravery, a man famous among the tribes. When they saw a youth of the youngest tribe of Israel, they were disappointed and refused him, notwithstanding that Samuel had anointed him and God had singled him out by lot.

It seemed as if God had understood the reason for the people's dislike of their new king, since it was customary for a king to have personal merit to recommend him. So, he caused a miracle, and Saul led the tribes to victory against the Ammonites. After the battle, all the people went

---

[23] Flavius Josephus (c. 37-65 AD) was a Roman-Jewish historian and a military leader, best known for writing *The Jewish War*.

to Gilgal and *"there they made Saul King before the Lord"*; that is, they accepted him.

¶ **44.** To all who assert unconditional obedience and claim that kings are made so by God, I say: there never was a king in the world that derived his authority from God alone. Saul, the first King of Israel, never sought to reign. It was the people who desired a king, even against the will of God. He was proclaimed king and lived a private life, looking after his father's cattle until he was made king the second time by the people at Gilgal.

Likewise, David, although he had been anointed by the God's command, was anointed the second time in Hebron by the tribe of Judaea and, after that, by all the people of Israel. A mutual covenant was made between him and them. A covenant lays an obligation upon kings and restrains them within bounds. All who reigned of David's posterity were appointed to the kingdom both by God and the people.

But I affirm, all other kings of any other country were made by the people only. It cannot be made to appear that kings are appointed by God in any other way than all other things, great or small, are appointed by him. The throne of David was in a peculiar manner called *The Throne of the Lord*, it being a type of our Saviour's everlasting throne in the Kingdom of Heaven from which line our Saviour proceeded. However, the thrones of princes are not God's, except in the sense that all other things in the world are His: *Thine, O Lord, is … all that is in Heaven, and in the Earth is thine. Both Riches and Honour come of thee, and thou reign over all*, Chronicles XXIX.

¶ **45.** When Solomon died, the people assembled themselves at Sichem to make Rehoboam, the son of Solomon, king. The people proposed conditions, upon which they were willing to admit him to the government. He asked for three days to seek advice. He consulted the old men and they persuaded him to comply with the people. Then he talked to the young men, who persuaded him to threaten the people with whips and scorpions and he answered the people as they advised him.

When all Israel saw that he would not listen to them, they openly declared against him and acknowledged the right of the people and their own liberty. It is confirmed to us that the right of choosing and changing their own government is, by the grant of God himself, in the people!

¶ **46.** David did not consider himself to be king before the tribe of Judaea had chosen him, and he often acknowledged Saul to be his Lord.

The word of God did not make him king, but only foretold that he should be king and prepared the hearts of the people to set him up. David, although designed by God to be king and anointed by the hand of the Prophet, was not king until the people had chosen him, and he had made a covenant with them. It will be hard to find a man who can claim a right which is not originally from the people.

If the people of Israel could elect and pull down, institute and abrogate, or even transfer to other persons, kingdoms more firmly established than any we know, the same right cannot be denied to any other nation. No other reason can be given for the infinite variety of constitutions in the world, other than the fact that the people who made them would have them so. **The rights and liberties of a nation may be utterly subverted and abolished if the power of the people may not be employed to assert those rights and liberties or punish the violation of them**.

It is the fundamental right of every nation to be governed by such laws, in such manner and by such persons as they think most conducive to their own good. The people are only accountable to themselves for what they do in that most important affair. The safety of all nations consists in rightly placing and measuring of power. The forever prospering nations are invariably those, who have given power to men from whom usurpations were least to be feared; who were least susceptible to be overcome, cheated or corrupted; and who, having the greatest interest in the nation, were most concerned to preserve its power, liberty and welfare. This is the greatest trust that can be placed in men.

The power of making, abrogating, changing, correcting, and interpreting laws is all-powerful. Kings have been rejected or deposed; the succession of the crown settled, regulated, or changed.

¶ **47.** Cicero, as translated by Sir Roger Lestrange: "*Herodotus* tells us, *that the Medians chose their Kings originally for the Probity of their Manners, and in hopes of enjoying the befits of common Justice*," which was the common practice of our predecessors. For whenever the weaker were oppressed by the stronger, the people presently selected another man, more excellent than the rest, for their protector. He was to relieve the distressed and to make such provisions that **common right might be done equally between all parties**. And, in the making of their laws, they had the same view as in the choice of their kings. **An equal and a common right was advocated without being qualified**. If the administration of one just man attained that goal, the people were content.

But, in case it failed, **there were laws which pronounce one and the same sentence to all and at all times**. In all elections, the people only cared for a prudent governor most revered for his justice. A nation would overcome all with a magistrate of such blameless conduct.

¶ **48.** The ancient Britons are historically described as fierce people, passionate for liberty, a free people who chose generals to command them in times of war, but who retained the government for themselves. They met armed in their general assemblies so that no decision would be forced on any of them. While smaller matters were left to the chieftains, they sought to resolve the most important issues themselves.

When the Romans invaded, they set up certain kings to govern the people in their territories. However, those who defended themselves, or retired to the north, or to the islands, were still governed by their own customs; they were never acquainted with domestic or foreign slavery. The Saxons, or Angli, were no less lovers of liberty, and understood the ways of defending it; they were certainly the most powerful and valiant people of Germany.

The ancient Britons and Saxons had no monarchs. Our ancestors had their councils and magistrates. As soon as the Saxons came into this country, they had their *Micklegemots*, i.e. general assemblies of the noble and free men, who had in themselves the power of the nation. We have historical evidence that **they resolved all matters according to their own pleasure**, which is **the utmost act of liberty and remains inviolable**.

We may be sure that those of the Norman race had no more power, since they swore to govern by the same laws. Their general councils were called *the general Council of the Bishops, Noblemen, Counts, all the wise Men, Elders, and people of the whole Kingdom*. In the time of Edward the Elder, they were called *the great Council of the Bishops, Abbots, Noblemen and People*. William of Malmsbury called them *the General Senate and Assembly of the People*. Sometimes they were called, *The Clergy and People*.

Regardless, all of them express **the same power, neither received from nor limited by kings**. Kings are said to be chosen or made and, sometimes, deposed, the reason being that those who institute magistracy best know whether the goals of the institution are rightly pursued or not. Their kings had no power but what was conferred upon them by the people. All just magistracies are the same in essence, though different in form; the same right will eternally belong to those who put the sovereign power into the hands of one or more men.

¶ **49.** The great historian Monsieur Mezeray gives this account of the ancient Germans: *There were, if I mistake not, three sorts of Government among the Germans. In some Places the People had the principal Authority, and yet they often elected a Prince, or a King; sometimes a General, whom we call Duke, from the Latin Word* Dux. *But the Power of these Chiefs descended entirely on the Community (the People) so that it was always a mixed Democracy. In other Parts among the Gothones, the Kings reigned with more Power, yet not to the Detriment of*

Liberty: **Their Royalty was limited by Laws, and the Reason of Things**. *As for Liberty, no People were ever so jealous of it, or ever defended it so long, and so successfully as the Germans. It may indeed be said, That Liberty being driven out of the best Part of the World by the* Roman *Arms, took Refuge on the further Side of the Rhine, where she had for her Companions and Guards, Poverty, Innocence, Frugality and Modesty, and where, in the Falseness of Woods and Morasses, sometimes on the defensive, and sometimes making courageous Sallies, She combated Five Hundred Years together against Tyranny, and all her Train, by which I mean Ambition, Luxury, Voluptuousness, Flattery, Corruption and Divisions, the Instruments which that cruel Enemy of human Race employs to forge Manacles and Chains.*

In the beginning of King William's reign, the aforesaid Monsieur, in discoursing on the difference of government in France and England, broke out saying, **Oh you most fortunate Englishmen!** *We had once in France the same Happiness, and the same Privileges which you have. Our Laws were made by Representatives of our own choosing; Our Money was not taken from us, but by our own Consent; Our Kings were subject to the Rules of Law and Reason. But now, alas! We are miserable and all is lost. Think nothing, Sir, too dear to maintain these precious Advantages! And if ever there be occasion, venture your Life, your Estate, and all you have, rather than submit to the Condition to which you see us reduced.*

¶ **50.** The election of magistrates was the original succession. The primary reason for people to associate themselves in a nation or kingdom was to be able to live in safety and to freely enjoy their property. They chose the best and wisest of their brethren as governors and trusted them with the administration of the country to achieve that goal.

Where the government was under a king, he usually held it for life and then, upon his demise the people proceeded to a new election to choose the most excellent man deserving of their trust. In gratitude to him, the people extended that honour to his heirs.

This is the just rise of succession. **Nothing but the consent of the governed can give a right to succession**. The next in succession to the crown of England was formerly reckoned to have a very precarious title. His good disposition and ability to sway the sceptre would recommend him to the affections of the people and, until the time of William the First, called the Conqueror, it was very common to break into the succession, and even to set aside all that family and line if it was expected that the public might suffer at their hand. For example, Cassibellan was not next in blood, yet was preferred before his elder brother's son, Egbert; Aethelstan, though a bastard and without any title, was elected by the consent of the nobility and people.

William, called the Conqueror, confessed in his last will that *he neither found, nor left the Kingdom as an Inheritance*.

If he possessed no right but what was conferred upon him, no more was conferred than had been enjoyed by the ancient kings, according to the approved laws which he swore to observe. Those laws gave no power to anyone before their election; and that which they then did give was so limited that the nobility and people reserved to themselves the resolving of the most important matters. They could even dismiss any who did not perform the duty of their Oaths and Office.

¶ **51.** After the Conquest in 1087, William Rufus, the second son of William the Conqueror, was elected. After his death, Henry I, his younger brother, was chosen by the people. **In his Charter, Henry acknowledged that he owed his crown to the Common Council of the Realm**.

Since Henry III's reign, the Succession has been altered several times, and the crown shifted from one family to another by an Act of Parliament.

There are numerous proofs of the power and authority of the people.

¶ **52.** Richard III was petitioned in the name of the three estates of parliament to accept the crown and at first modestly refused. However, afterwards he said, "*We well perceive, that all the Realm is so set,* … **whom no Earthly Man can govern against their Wills**, *and also we perceive, that no Man there is, to whom the Crown can by just Title appertain, as to our self, as very right Heir, lawfully begotten of our most dear Father,* Richard, *late Duke of York, …."*

An Act of Parliament was then passed to establish King Richard III's lawful election.

¶ **53.** A clause in King Henry's Charter says, **If the King invades those Rights**, (meaning the rights of the people) **it is lawful for the Kingdom to raise against him, and to do him what Injury they can, as though they owed him no Allegiance**.

By an Act of Parliament of the 12th [year] of Richard II, it was enacted, **That if the King, through a foolish Obstinacy, and Contempt of his People, or perverse forward Will, or by any other irregular Way, shall alienate himself from his People, and will not be governed and regulated by the Rights of the Kingdom, and laudable Ordinances made by the Council of the Lords, and great Men of the Realm, but fall headily in his mad Councils, exercise his own arbitrary Will; from thenceforth it is lawful for them, with the common Assent and Consent of the People of the Realm, to abrogate or depose him from the Throne, and set up in his stead, somebody of Kin, or near of Kin to the King of the Royal Stock.**

This gives a lot of leeway for choosing a deserving person of the royal stock.

¶ **54.** By the Acts of Parliament of the 25th and 28th years of Henry the VIII's reign, it is declared that *"if … no Provision [is] made in the King's Life time, who should rule and govern this Realm, then the Realm shall be destitute of a lawful Governor."*

¶ 55. The Act of the 13th year of Elizabeth's reign makes it treason to deny the power of parliament to limit or alter the succession, and includes a penalty for those who affirm, *"That any but the Issue of the Queen's Body had Right to succeed after her."*

¶ 56. King Alfred acknowledged in his will that *he owed his Crown to the Bounty of his Princes and of the Elders of his People.*

¶ 57. The power which the people of England had in the disposal of the crown during the time of the Saxons is confirmed to us by the noble record of Sir Henry Spelman[24], *That … in Calebuth, Anno 787, it was ordained and enacted, that the King should be elected by Parliament and, being chosen, he should have prudent Councillors fearing God.*

This right over the crown, which our ancestors exercised in the time of the Saxons, has been maintained and used with courage and vigour in every age since the coming of the Normans.

¶ 58. William I, who is unjustly styled the Conqueror, having subdued Harold and those who abetted him, obtained the crown by the free choice of the peers and the body of the people. Before his coronation, he was made to swear that he would govern the people justly and keep and observe all their old laws and consent for the enacting of further laws, as might be needed for the preservation and prosperity of the realm.

¶ 59. The famous Lawyer Bracton said, ***"in governing the People, the King has above him the Law, by which he is constituted King,***

---

[24] Henry Spelman was a long-standing member of parliament and sat on several royal councils, including the Council for New England (from 1620). He authored the famous *Concilia Ecclesiastica Orbis Britannici (1639)*, referred to here.

41

and his Parliament, viz. *The Earls and Barons … wherefore if the King becomes lawless, they must give him Law, and curb him*." When speaking of curbing a king who is in arms to oppress the state, it is obvious that he should be forced to either renounce his tyrannical ways or leave the Land.

¶ 60. Bracton further says[25]: ***The King does no Wrong, as he does nothing but by Law***. And that ***The Power of the King is the Power of the Law; a Power of Right, not of Wrong***. Also: ***If the King does Injustice, he is not King***.

The King therefore ought to exercise the power of the Law, *as becomes the Vicar and Minister of God upon Earth; because that Power is the Power of God alone; but the Power of doing Wrong is the Power of the Devil, and not of God; and the King is his Minister, whose Work he does. Whilst he does Justice, he is the Vicar of the Eternal King; but if he deflects from it, to act unjustly, he is the Minister of the Devil.*

Bracton also says that the King is ***Master of none, servant to all***.

¶ 61. In the Laws of Edward the Confessor, which he collected and observed strictly as Laws of the Kingdom, it is written "***That the King ought to do all Things in his Kingdom according to Law, and by the Judgment of his Peers***." St. Edward's Law goes further: that unless the king performs his duty, for which he was elected, he would be king in name only.

¶ 62. William Rufus and Henry I got the consent of the people by promising to grant them their usual laws and ancient customs.

---

[25] Referring to his work *De legibus et consuetudinibus Angliæ (The Laws and Customs of England)*

If any king refused to do so, the nobles would hinder his coronation until he made this promise. Henry IV, V, and VI were only kings by Acts of Parliament. It appears that the kings of England were kings only by virtue of a contract between themselves and the people. This is apparent by the contract that the nobles and commons of England made with the Conqueror.

¶ **63.** Florence of Worcester, Simon of Durham, and R. Howden[26] specifically say, *"William, called the Conqueror, made a League, or Compact, with the Arch-Bishops, Bishops, Earls, and Nobles of the Land, who met him at Bercham, and swore Fealty to him, so he reciprocally, being required so to do by the Arch-Bishop of York,* **made his personal Oath** *before the Altar of St. Peter,* **To defend the Holy Church of God, and the Rectors of the same, to govern all the People subject to him justly, to establish equal Laws, and to see them duly executed."**

His secretary, Ingulphus, said, *"That the Laws of King Edward the Confessor should be perpetual, authentical, and be observed inviolably through the whole Kingdom of England"*.

R. Howden said further, *"He [i.e. William the Conqueror] commanded* **the Laws of King Edward to be observed in all things:** *And that, in the Fourth Year of his Reign, by the Counsel of his Barons, he made the noble and wise Men of England to be summoned throughout all the Provinces of England, that he might hear from them who were skilled in their Law, their rights and Customs and that Twelve Men were chosen out of every County, who swore, to their Power, to tread in a right Path, neither turning to the right Hand, or to the Left, and to make known to him the Custom and the Establishment of their Laws."*

¶ **64.** Henry I and Stephen, who succeeded Henry, entered a contract and promised an amendment of the Laws.

---

[26] Roger of Howden (appointed 1169 - died 1202) was an English chronicler and diplomat, who served as a Minister of Howden, Yorkshire.

¶ **65.** **The original Compact was,** said M. Paris, *that the King should govern them according to the Tenor of such ancient Laws and original Customs, as were received among them, according to the good, approved, and ancient Laws of the Kingdom.*

All kings have stated in one form or another that they would observe and govern in accordance with *The Laws of* England, also known as *the ancient Laws of this Realm, originally established.*

In our Statutes these are referred to as *The Laws of the Land.*

In his Oath, Richard II said *The Good Laws of the Land.*

King John called them *The Charters of the Liberties of* England, or *the Common Liberty.*

Henry III famously said: *The fundamental Laws of the Kingdom, let it be observed.*

It certainly appears, **by the Oaths taken at their Coronations, that they meant to protect the People's ancient Rights, Liberties, original Customs and Laws, and govern by the Laws of the country. The People have continuously claimed the Laws of the Land, the Laws of King Edward, and *Magna Carta*, as their Right.** Our ancestors thought it absolutely necessary that whoever would be their King should enter into a contract with them and be as much engaged to keep their privileges as they were to keep their allegiance to him. Commonly, the king was sworn before the people would engage to be his subjects. It is reasonable, then, that as he continues to be their king, he should keep his Oaths and protect the people's privileges for which they, in turn, should continue in their allegiance.

When these *Patria Leges*, these ancient laws of the country, were violated, the people would immediately complain of the injustice and if they could not prevail by fair means, they would quit their subjection and fight to recover their right by arms. In short, this oath and compact is the very ground and cause of the oath of allegiance. The Lord Chancellor Fortescue declared justly that **our kings are political kings, who receive their power from the people.**

¶ **66.** Grotius[27] said, "*Succession alone does not denominate the Manner or specify the particular Form of the Governor, but is only a Continuation of that Right which was first settled, and as much as was first given, is afterwards continued by Succession, and no more.*" So, we may reasonably infer that succession only gives kings what the first election ever gave them, **making them kings by contract**, having agreed to the conditions set out at the first time their predecessors accepted to exercise royal authority.

¶ **67.** In the year 1253, a full parliament was assembled, where King Henry III promised faithfully to ratify the Magna Carta and observe all its articles, as he had sworn to do at his coronation. This was done in the most solemn and ceremonial manner. The King and all the great nobility of England, all the Bishops and chief Prelates in their ornaments, with burning candles in their hands, assembled to hear the terrible sentence of excommunication on all infringers of the Oath.

At the lighting of the candles, the king gave his to one of the prelates, saying, "*It becomes not me, who am no Priest, to hold this Candle; my Heart shall be a greater Testimony*", and laid his hand on his breast the whole time the sentence was being read *in the Name of the Omnipotent God, etc.* When done, the Charter of King John, his Father, was read.

In the end, having thrown away their candles, they cried out, "*So let them who incur this Sentence be extinct, and flunk in Hell*". The King with a loud voice said, "*As God help me, I will, as a Man, a Christian, a Knight, a King Crowned and anointed, inviolably observe all these Things.*"

Notwithstanding all this, the king broke his oath the very next year, 1263, by continuing to govern contrary to the Charter. The barons waged war on him under the command of Simon of Montfort, who succeeded in taking the king and his sons prisoners, but the prince escaped, fought with Simon, and slew him. The historians of those times

---

[27] Hugo Grotius wrote the book *De Jure Belli ac Paci* (1625) *On the Law of War and Peace,* arguing that war is justifiable only if a country faces imminent danger and the use of force is both necessary and proportionate to the threat.

called Simon a most devout servant of God and Church, and a most faithful Protector, Shield, and Defender of the kingdom of England. He was declared a martyr for the Liberties of Church and State.

At the end of the war, in 1269, a parliament was held at Marlborough, where the **Statutes of Marlborough** were enacted. In their fifth chapter, it is decreed that *"The Great Charter and the Charter de Forresta[28] shall be observed in all their Articles, both concerning the King and his Subjects."* Lord Coke later observed that *"after this Parliament, neither Magna Carta, nor Carta de Forresta, was ever attempted to be impugned, or questioned, whereupon Peace and Tranquillity have since ensued."*

¶ 68. Magna Carta is only a summary of our ancient laws and customs. The king who swears to it swears to them all and is not allowed to be their interpreter, or to determine what is good or evil, what to be observed or annulled. He can have no more power over the rest of us. Since then, this has been confirmed by more parliaments than we have had kings. All of them have the same obligation as John and Henry, in whose time that claim of right was compiled. We know the value of our liberties and the courage with which our ancestors defended them, and we can have no better example to encourage us never to suffer them violated or diminished.

¶ 69. The nobility of England, as the Lord Coke observes, have always held the Laws of England in great esteem and reverence, and would never allow them to be changed. This made Henry I write the following to Pope Paschal[29]: *"Let your Holiness know, that, by the help of God, whilst I live,* **the Dignities and Customs of our Kingdom of England shall**

---

[28] The Forest Charter was issued in 1217 as a complementary annex to the Magna Cart 1215. It formally allowed all free men access to the royal forests. It was re-issued in 1225, which copy of is held by the British Library today. As a result of this Charter, the size of the royal forests was reduced and claimed for farmland.

[29] Reference to Pope Paschal II, who ruled the papal states between 1099 and 1118.

not be diminished, and if I, which God forbid, should so far deject myself, my Nobles, and **all the People of England, would never suffer them to be altered.**"

¶ **70.** The nobility of England, with the assent of the whole commonalty assembled in Parliament at Lincoln, wrote to Pope *Boniface*, "*By Virtue of our Oath,* **we are bound to the Observation and Defence of the Liberties, Customs, and the Laws of our Country,** *which by the help of God, we will defend with our whole Power; nor do we permit our Lord, the King, even if he were willing, to attempt things so unusual, undue, and prejudicial to the Royal Dignity*". Their letter was sealed by 104 earls and barons in the name of all the commons of England.

¶ **71.** King John received the crown by election, as he was chosen by the states. M. Paris[30] said, "*All consented to the Speech of the Archbishop, that none ought to succeed another in the Kingdom, unless he were Elected by the Community, and thereupon they Elected the Count, and took him for their King*".

¶ **72.** King James in his fourth speech at Whitehall in 1609 said that the King was *Lex Loquens*[31], after a fashion, binding himself by a double oath to the adherence to the fundamental laws of his kingdom tacitly, because as king he is bound to protect both the people and the laws of his kingdom, and expressly by his Coronation Oath as every just king in any kingdom is bound to observe the pact made to his people by his laws and by suitably framing his government.

Therefore, a king governing in a settled kingdom ceases to be a king and degenerates into a tyrant as soon as he abandons the laws. All non-

---

[30] Reference to the English monk and chronicler Matthew of Paris (c. 1200-1259)

[31] From the Latin maxim: *Ludex est lex loquens,* meaning "The judge is the Law speaking", i.e. the judge alone can declare what the law is and how it applies to the facts of the case.

tyrannical kings are glad to confine themselves within the limits of the laws, while those who persuade them to the contrary are vipers and pests.

¶ 73. As the subjects of the king are born to lands and other things, so are they born to inherit and enjoy the laws of this realm, so that every man has an equal benefit by Law.

This is called common right and is a greater inheritance to every man than that which descends to him from his parents, because thereby his goods, lands, wife, children, his body, life, honour, and value are all protected from injury and wrong.

This common right is called the law of the subject, and the judges are sworn to execute justice according to the law and custom of England. **All this proves how justly the laws are called the great inheritance of every subject; it is the inheritance of inheritances, without which we have no inheritance.** The king's prerogative is law, too, because, as it was resolved, the **king has no prerogative but that which the law of the land allows him.** The law says: the king is the fountain of justice and all justice done within the realm is said to flow from this fountain. It must, however, always run within the known conduits of the law.

¶ 74. Glanville[32], who was a learned lawyer and Chief Justice in Henry II's days over 500 years ago, wrote a book of the common laws of England. His is the most ancient of any existing on the subject. It informs us that there was, in his time, such a thing as high treason against the kingdom. In his words, **a crime in law is a crime committed by the magistrates as it annihilates the law of the king and the kingdom.**

---

[32] Ranulf de Glanville, Chief Minister of England (1180-89) was the reputed author of the first authoritative text on common law: *Tractatus de legibus et consuetudinibus regni Angliae*

¶ **75.** Those who flatter a king that he is above the law most notoriously contradict one of the first axioms of our regal government, namely, **_Lex facit Regem_**[33]. The king subjects himself to the law by his Coronation Oath.

It proves that a king of England is king by law, since the first monarch was made so by consent, and the Coronation Oath is a fundamental law of this kingdom, which precedes the subject's oath of fealty. He is a legal king, his authority is legal and, as Fortescue says, his royal power is restrained by the power politic[34].

Therefore, a king's grant of any favour made contrary to law is void, according to another axiom of our government, **_The king can do nothing save what he can lawfully do_**. It is the very essence of our kings to govern according to law, for where the will governs, and not the law, there he is no longer a king. **The Law is to be the only rule and measure of his government.** On this basis, it is said that a king of England can do no wrong, nor will his prerogative allow him to do an injury to anyone.

¶ **76.** It is ordained and established that henceforth **the King can neither send letters or use the signet, or the king's privy seal if it is in damage or prejudice of the realm, or if it is contrary to the Law.**

¶ **77.** During Richard II's reign, Tresillian[35] and five judges, along with a man from the king's council at law, delivered their extravagant, illegal and extra-judicial opinions that the king might avoid a statute, ordinance,

---

[33] From Latin: The King is subject to the Law. The full maxim states _Rex non debet esse sub homine, sed sub Deo et sub lege, quia lex facit regem_ which means "The king is subject to the law, because it is the law which makes him king".

[34] Reference to Sir John Fortescue's notable legal treatise _De Laudibus Legum Anglia_ (In Praise of the Laws of England) c. 1470

[35] Reference to the infamous Sir Robert Tresillian who became Lord Chief Justice in the time of Richard II

and commission, made for the safety of both king and kingdom in parliament by the peers and commons of the land and with the king's assent. They were all executed as traitors by the judgment of the most supreme court of judicature in the kingdom, the parliament.

¶ **78.** It is declared in the historical records, "***The King has no Prerogative that derogates from Justice and Equity.***" Bracton said, "***The Regal Power is according to Law. He has no Power to do any Wrong, nor can the King do any thing but what the Law warrants.***"

Our most authoritative records declare, "***That our Kings owe all their Power, not to any Right of Inheritance of Conquest, or Succession, but to the People.***" So, in the parliament rolls of Henry IV, we read, ***That the Kingly Office and Power was granted by the Commons to King Henry IV, and before him to his Predecessor, Richard II.*** Because he abused it to the subversion of the law, contrary to his oath at his coronation, the same people who granted him power took it back and deposed him.

This and other examples plainly show that the kingly office is nothing but a trust and a gift by ***Vox Populi***[36] of all the people by their delegates in parliament assembled.

¶ **79.** In an ordinary monarchy, such as in Germany and England, **the kings can neither make nor change the laws. They are under the Law, and the Law is not under them**. Their letters or commands are not binding. In the administration of justice, the question is not what pleases them, but what the Law declares to be right, which must have its course, whether the king be busy or at leisure. The king never dies and is always present in the supreme courts.

---

[36] Latin: "the voice of the people". The full phrase is *Vox populi, vox Dei*, meaning "The voice of the people is God's voice".

¶ **80.** We have had no tougher king than Henry VIII and yet even he acknowledged that the power of making, changing, and repealing laws is with parliament. It wasn't him but parliament that dissolved the abbeys. He did not take their lands to himself, but received what parliament thought fit to give him. He did not reject the supremacy of the pope, nor assume any other power in spiritual matters, other than what parliament conferred to him.

¶ **81. The judges of the land** are chosen by the king on the advice of his council, yet are so far from depending on his will **that they swear faithfully to serve the people as well as the king, and to do justice to every man according to the law of the land, notwithstanding any writs, letters or commands received from him, and, in default thereof, they are to forfeit their bodies, lands, and goods as in cases of treason.**

Queen Elizabeth and her counsellors pressed the judges to obey her great seal in the case of Cavendish, but they answered: *That both she and they had taken an Oath to keep the Law, and if they should obey her Commands, the Law would not warrant them.* In addition to the offence against God, country, and the commonwealth, they alleged the example of Empson and Dudley[37], who were executed as traitors (as were Gaveston, Tresillian, and others) for subverting the laws of the land in obedience to the king's command, saying that "*they were deterred from obeying her illegal Commands.*"

Those who had sworn to keep the Law, notwithstanding the king's writs, knew that the Law depended not upon his will.

According to *Magna Carta*, **judgments are to be passed by equals. No man can be imprisoned, disseized[38] of his freehold, or deprived of life or limb, unless by sentence of his peers.** Bracton says that *"in*

---

[37] Executed in 1509, just after the death of Henry VII. They were famous for collecting debts owed to the king, requesting bonds as surety and employing other financial instruments.

[38] Deprived of possession or freehold interest, especially wrongfully or by force.

receiving justice the King is equal to another Man". This could not be if judgments were given by him or if he were exempted from judgment by **the very Law, which has put all judgements into the hands of the people. This power is executed by the people in grand or petty juries, and the judges are assistants to them** in explaining the difficult points of the Law, in which it is presumed they should be learned.

The strength of every judgement is in the verdict of these juries. The judges do not give but only pronounce or declare a verdict. By law, a jury verdict given contrary to the advice or direction of the judges is acceptable. However, that same law exposes the judges to penalties if, upon their own heads or a command from the king, they presume to give sentence without or contrary to a verdict. No pretentions to the power of interpreting the Law can exempt them if they break it. Even in special verdicts, the judges are only assistants to the juries, and the verdict is from the juries though the judges, having heard the point argued, declare the meaning of the relevant Law.

¶ 82. First Act[39] of *William* and *Mary*, **declaring the Rights and Liberties of the Subject, and settling the Succession of the Crown**. In the first place, as their ancestors have usually done, for the vindicating and asserting their ancient rights and liberties, they declare:

I. *That the pretended Power of suspending or execution of Laws by Regal Authority without Consent of Parliament is illegal.*

II. *That the pretended Power of dispersing or execution of Laws by Regal Authority as it has been assumed and exercised of late is illegal.*

[39] The current version of this Act is but a faint echo of the original text, cited here. See https://www.legislation.gov.uk/aep/WillandMar/1/1

III. *That the Commission for instituting the late Court of Commissioners for Ecclesiastical Causes[40] and all other Commissions and Courts of like Nature are illegal and pernicious.*

IV. *That levying Money for the Use of the Crown by Pretence of Prerogative, without Grant of Parliament for longer Time, or in another Manner than the same is granted, is illegal.*

V. *That it is the Right of the Subjects to Petition[41] the King, and all Commitments and Prosecutions for such Petitioning are illegal.*

VI. *That the raising or keeping a Standing Army within the Kingdom in time of Peace, unless it be with Consent of Parliament, is against Law.*

VII. *That the Subjects who are Protestant may have Arms for their Defence, according to their Conditions and as allowed by Law.*

VIII. *That Election of Members of Parliament ought to be free.*

IX. *That the Freedom of Speech, and Debates, or Proceedings in Parliament, ought not to be impeached or questioned in any Court or Place out of Parliament.*

X. *That excessive Bail ought not to be required, nor excessive Fines imposed, nor cruel and unusual Punishments inflicted.*

XI. *That Jurors ought to be impanelled and returned, and Jurors who pass judgement upon Men in trials for High Treason ought to be Freeholders.*

XII. *That all Grants and Promises of Fines and Forfeitures of particular Persons before Conviction are illegal and void.*

---

[40] The Ecclesiastical Commission of 1868 was in effect a revival of the Court of High Commission, declared illegal by the Long Parliament during the reign of Charles I by the Triennial Act, and was intended by James II as a means to move England back towards Catholicism by sanctioning those hostile to it. Source: Wikipedia

[41] From the Latin verb *petere* meaning "to lay claim to"; and the Anglo-Norman word *peticiun* meaning "request, demand"

XIII. *And that for Redress of all Grievances, and for the amending, strengthening, and preserving of the Laws, Parliaments ought to be held frequently.*

They claim, demand and insist upon all and singular the above premises as their undoubted rights and liberties. No declarations, judgments, acts, or proceedings to the prejudice of the people in any of the said premises can have any legal consequence.

Further, experience has shown that it is inconsistent with the safety and welfare of this protestant kingdom to be governed by a king or queen of the Roman Catholic faith and, therefore, the latter will be excluded from the royal succession. The crown and government can only be enjoyed by protestants.

¶ **83.** It must be clear by now that **all government, authority and magistracy proceed from the people**. Next, I will show that the people have authority to set aside an heir to government when unfit or uncapable to govern. Also, they can dispossess them if they fail to observe the laws by which and for which their dignities were given them. When done in just and urgent causes and by public authority of the whole nation, the justice done is obvious.

If a prince endeavours to establish a religion repugnant to Scripture, contrary to the laws of the land, or aims to destroy the people, or endeavours to make them slaves to his tyrannical will and pleasure, then just as the human body may cure its head when out of order, so may the body politic purge its head, when pernicious or destructive to it. A civil body may have different heads by succession or election and cannot be bound to one, as a human body is.

If a body had the ability to cut off its aching head and take another, would it not do it? All men would confess it had sufficient authority and reason to do so, rather than let the other parts perish or live in pain and incessant torment. Equally, the body politic may choose another head and governor to replace its destructive one. This has been done for many ages and God has wonderfully concurred with such judicial acts of the commonwealth against their evil princes by providing some notable successor in place of the deprived.

¶ **84.** Long is the list of all the kings of Israel, whom God permitted to be slain, as well as those that were carried away captive by the heathens for their unjust government. Let us now leave the Hebrews and look at several examples of evil princes deprived of government in France, Spain, Portugal and, last of all, in Scotland and England. Happiness and prosperity accompanied those proceedings showing God's approval of such acts.

¶ **85.**

There were two great changes made of the royal line in France: the first from Pharamond to the line of Pepin, where the most remote in blood descendants were preferred before the nearest and bastards before the legitimate heirs; the second was from Pepin to Hugo Capet, in which family the crown remains to this day. Childerick III was deprived for his evil government and Pepin was chosen king in his stead, whose posterity reigned after him for many years and were brave kings, as history testifies.

Louis III and Charles, surnamed *Le Gross*, were both deposed by the states of France for their evil government, and more worthy were appointed in their stead. All French historians attribute the prosperity and greatness of their kingdom to these great changes made by the people.

¶ **86.** In Spain, Rotherick and Alphonso were deposed for evil government. Bernard, the son of Charlemaine of France, was rejected because the Spaniards would not be governed by a Frenchman. Alphonso III, surnamed *The Great*, fell into tyranny and was twice deposed. Favila, King of Castile, a cruel tyrant, was deposed by the Castilians.

Alphonso IV was judged unfit to govern and was made to surrender the kingdom to his brother Ramicus. Ordonius usurped the crown and banished Santius Crasius, but the people rose to restore their good king, pulled down Ordonius, and reinstated Santius.

Blanch, Wife of Louis XVIII of France, was rejected and Sister Beringaria was raised in her stead. Alphonso X was deposed; Flavio Suintilla was overthrown for his evil government and *Sissinando* was chosen in his place.

Peter *The Cruel* was twice dethroned and the second time they sent for his half-brother Henry, bastard to Alphonso, the eleventh King of Castile. This Henry was a most excellent king and was famous for his bravery and courage in war.

¶ **87.** In 1581 the states of Holland, in a general assembly at the Hague, abjured all obedience and subjection to Phillip, King of Spain, and justified it in a declaration: *For that by his tyrannous Government, against Faith so often given and broken, he had lost his Right to all the Belgic Provinces; that therefore they deposed him.* From that time to this, no state or kingdom has prospered as much as Holland.

¶ **88.** In Portugal, Alphonsus was deposed because he was young, and his mother was encroaching on the people's liberties. Don Sancho II was deprived by the universal consent of all Portugal, and Don Alanso, his brother, was set up. Amongst other great exploits, he was the first to set Portugal free from all subjection, dependence, and homage to the kingdom of Castile. His son, who was his successor and a most rare prince, built and founded about forty great towns in Portugal. His offspring rules to this day.

¶ **89.** In Denmark, Christopher II, Waldemar, and Erich were deposed for their evil government; in 1523 when Christian II was deposed for evil government, Frederick, Duke of Holstein, was chosen in his stead. The present king of Denmark, *Osternus*, was overthrown for his intolerable cruelty, and his three children disinherited.

¶ **90.** In Poland, Lecticus II, Lescus I, Miccislauus, Senior, and Vladislaus III, surnamed Locticus, were deposed for their maladministration. Sigismond was refused the Crown, though heir to it, because he was a Hungarian. Henry of Anjou deserted Poland when he was made King of France, so they chose a new king.

¶ **91.** In Sweden, Ingellus, Amund, Swercher, Waldimar, Birgir, Magnus, and Albert, his Successor, were all twice deposed; Erick was twice deposed and Christopher, Duke of Bavaria, was made king in his stead; Charles Cnateson was deposed and Christian King of Denmark was crowned in his stead, who later turned tyrant and was deposed.

Stensture, who reigned fourteen years as regent, not king, was deposed and John II was made king, who turning tyrant, was also deposed and Stensture was made regent again.

¶ **92.** Tarquin was expelled for his tyranny. The Romans had such a hatred against his whole family that they would never after name any of their children Tarquin. Upon the alteration of their government, Junius Brutus was made consul and personally executed justice on his own sons, seeing them put to death for conspiring to restore the family of Tarquin to the throne.

Among others, Romulus, Numa Pompilius, and Tarquinius Superbus were deposed for their tyranny, and the Roman government turned into the best regulated commonwealth that the world had ever seen.

The deposing of Roman Emperors would be endless to enumerate. None of them could pretend to have any divine right, especially since most were of modest birth and proclaimed soldiers. Valentinian was the son of a roper; Jovian was of penurious birth and a foot soldier, and so on. They rose by force and were driven out by force, and thirty-six of them murdered each another. History is full of examples of this kind and the nearer we go back to the beginning of government, the more instances we have of the peoples setting up and pulling down their monarchs for tyranny.

¶ **93.** The emperors of Germany, when they infringed the rules of government, which they had sworn inviolably to observe, or violated the fundamental laws of the empire, were opposed and resisted and finally deprived of the empire. The German Lawyers have always held, and still hold it for a certain truth, that *when they abuse their Power, for the overturning of the State, or for invading the Rights of the Princes of the Empire, that it is a Right inherent in the Empire, to deprive them of their imperial Dignity and to confer it on another.* This is declared by Lampadius, Arnizaus, Diderick, Cenringius, Lambert, Schasnaburgh, Aventin, Cuspin, and many others. Louis the Good was deposed in 833; in 1400 Henry IV and Wenceslaus were deposed for their evil government of the empire.

¶ **94.** In Scotland, the nobility and gentry took arms against their king Durstius for his intolerable cruelty, slew him in battle, and elected Even, his brother, in his stead.

Cratby Cinthus, having surprised and slain Donald for his tyranny, was unanimously chosen King. Ethus was deprived for his evil government and Gregory made king in his stead. James III of Scotland was deserted and slain for endeavouring to introduce an arbitrary government after violating many solemn promises to the contrary. In a free parliament, called soon after the Battle of the Field of Stirling was fully debated, and by the unanimous consent of the three estates, it was declared and adjudged *That those that were slain in the said Field of Stirling, in the Assistance and Defence of the late King, had fallen by their own deserving, and justly suffered the Punishment of their Rashness.*

By an Act of Parliament, the arbitrary proceedings of the said King James III were condemned, fines and forfeits imposed on the nobility and gentry that stood by him at the Battle of Stirling, and all those that fought against him in defence of their laws and liberties were justified and cleared. This is printed in the Scottish Acts of Parliament, by the authority of Queen Mary of Scotland. In his *History of the Five James*, Buchanan said that the people were free from the beginning and only created kings on the very condition that ***the Empire being conferred on them by the Suffrages of the People, if the Matter required it, they might take it away by the same Suffrages***. To date, much evidence is available of this fact.

¶ **95.**   Finally, let us look at examples from England: Archigallo, Emerian, Vortigern, Sigibert, King of the West Saxons, Beornred, and Alured, King of Northumberland, were all deprived of their thrones for evil government. Men who were thought more worthy were favoured in their stead. The crown of the deposed King Edwin was given to his brother Edgar, who was one of the best princes the world had at the time in both peace and war, a man of justice, piety, and valour. According to Stow[42], he kept a substantial navy fleet of 3,600 ships and he built and restored forty-seven monasteries at his own expense.

¶ **96.**   After the Conquest, King Edward II, Richard II, and Richard III were deprived of their crown for not governing according to the Laws of the Land. Edward III and Henry IV and VII were elected in their place and proved most rare and valiant princes. They were responsible for many important changes in the kingdom, including altering the course of descent of the royal blood line. According to the doctrine of passive obedience without reserve, if the changes and deprivations of

---

[42] John Stow (1525-1605), an English historian and antiquarian, who published *The Chronicles of England* and *The Annales of England*.

the former kings were unlawful, these changes would have been unjust and void to this day so, consequently, all those who succeeded them would have been usurpers. However, the pretenders to the crown of England today have no title but by virtue of an Act of Parliament, as they are descended from the men replacing those deposed by the People.

It is and always has been the custom and practice of all kingdoms and commonwealths to dethrone their princes for evil government and the fact that God concurs is plain from the above examples of the prosperity and happiness resulting from those acts.

¶ 97. In the reign of the treacherous King John, the barons, prelates, and commons took a solemn oath to wage war on the king if he refused to formally confirm their laws and liberties. If he were to then break his royal oath, he would be brought down, and his castles forfeit.

He did indeed break his oath and promises, so the barons decided that "he should be expelled from the throne" and no longer be permitted to rule. They sent a delegation of lords and commoners beyond the sea to invite Louis, the prince of France, to be their king and promised to swear fealty to him.

However, it became clear that Louis had plans to oppress and uproot them, so they chose Henry III, King John's eldest son, who was hardly nine years old at the time. The great marshal, earl of Pembroke, convinced them that the son should not be held responsible for the iniquities of his father. At last, the whole council unanimously accepted him and set a date for his coronation.

¶ 98. In the reign of Edward II, the parliament met at London and, by common consent, declared him unworthy of the crown. They chose his son Edward by unanimous consent and his election was publicly declared in Westminster Hall. Edward II was told of his son's election and was made to resign the crown. All the people and all the prelates consented to the election, and the Archbishop urged them to declare for the King Elect reminding them, ***Vox Populi, Vox Dei***.

¶ **99.** In the 39th year of Henry VI's reign, Richard, Duke of York, laid his claim to the crown in parliament. Long arguments and deliberations followed among the peers, prelates, and commons of the realm. Finally, it was agreed that Henry should remain as king, but if he died or resigned of his own accord or infringed any point of the royal contract, the crown would revert to the Duke of York.

These Articles of Agreement were written down, sealed and sworn to by the two parties, and enacted in the High Court of Parliament.

The duke Richard was slain in the battle of Wakefield, so his son Edward called a council of the Lords Spiritual and Temporal and laid open his title to the realm by the Articles of Agreement. The Lords considered his title and declaration and determined the following:

King Henry VI has infringed the order enacted by parliament, acting contrary to his oath, honour, and agreement. Also, as he was inefficient to rule the realm and unprofitable to the commonwealth, he was by the same authority, deprived and rejected of all kingly honour and regal sovereignty. Edward, earl of Marche, was named, elected, and admitted for king and governor of the realm by the lords in the said council assembled.

As the people got together in St. John's fields that day, the Lord Fauconbridge wisely declared to the multitude the offences and breaches of the late agreement committed by King Henry VI and asked them if they would have King Henry to reign any longer over them. The crowd shouted *No!* Then he asked them if they would serve and obey the earl of Marche as their sovereign lord and the crowd clapped their hands and answered *Yes!*

The lords witnessed the loving consent of the commons, frankly and freely given. The earl was told of this development and the next day it was conveyed to Westminster. The earl's title and claim to the crown was declared: first, as Richard's son and heir and, second, by authority of parliament and the forfeiture committed by King Henry. He was then crowned king at Westminster by the name of King Edward IV.

¶ **100. Thus, by the common usage of England and the common law[43], kings degenerating into tyrants may be deposed for evil government and others set up in their stead**.

¶ **101. That all magistrates and governors proceed from the people** is plain from the following examples in Scripture, Deuteronomy XVI. 18, 19: *The Children of Israel are commanded to make Judges and Officers throughout their Tribes*. Deuteronomy XVII. 14, 15. .... ***You shall set one from amongst your brethren over yourselves; you may not set a Stranger to rule over you***.

So, God only reserved to himself the nomination of their king to make his people happier. Knowing the heart of man and man's nature, he nominated those who were most fit to govern his people. Yet God did not require the Jews to accept his nominee for king but left it to their own free will to decide if they would approve of him or not.

When Saul died, David was set up by the appointment of Almighty God, yet only the tribe of Judaea followed David and made him king. Eleven tribes followed Ishbosheth, Saul's son. David fought a long war against them, yet he never called them rebels; neither did God punish them or send any judgment upon them for not accepting David as king. When Ishbosheth was killed, all tribes came to David and negotiated a contract

---

[43] Common law is defined in the Oxford Dictionary 1933 edition as "the unwritten law of England, administered by the King's courts, which purports to be derived from ancient usage, and is embodied in the older commentaries and the reports of abridged cases". The term, which is now used synonymously with "law of the land", originated with the legal reforms of Henry II in the twelfth century and was called "common" because it applied equally throughout the country. Source: https://www.iclr.co.uk/knowledge/topics/the-english-legal-system/

with him, including conditions to secure their Liberty, before they made him king.

¶ **102.** Solomon was made king by David, his father. This was insufficient without the people's consent, so, finally, the people anointed Solomon and confirmed him as king.

¶ **103.** Saul left behind many children, but only Ishbosheth succeeded him. Another of his sons, Jonathan, was slain in war and copiously praised in holy Scripture. His other son Mephibosheth did not succeed to the crown, though by succession he had a more credible right to it than David. God promised David, *"that his Seed Should Reign for ever after"*. He was succeeded by Solomon, his tenth and youngest son.

After Solomon's death, Rehoboam, the lawful son and heir of King Solomon, went to Shechem, where all the people of Israel were assembled for his coronation and admission to the crown. He refused to ease the heavy taxes imposed by his father, so ten of the twelve tribes refused to accept him as their king and chose Jeroboam, his servant, instead. They made him their lawful king and God allowed it. When Rehoboam prepared an army to subdue the ten tribes to his obedience, God commanded him to desist, and so he did. Ammon was slain by his own servants, but the people of the land slew the conspirators and made Josiah, his son, king in his stead.

¶ **104.** In *Judges* VIII 21-23, Gideon refused to be made king, so the Children of Israel chose his illegal son Abimelech for their king, even though Gideon had seventy lawfully born ones.

¶ **105.** Zimri assassinated Afa, the king of Judaea, and reigned in his stead. However, when the Children of Israel heard of it, they rejected him and made Omri, the Captain of the Host, King of Israel, *Kings* XVI 15-16.

¶ **106.** The Israelites met and chose Ehud, Gideon, Sampson, Jephthah, and others to be their leaders because they judged them fit to defeat their enemies. By the same right, they assembled at Mispeth to wage war against the tribe of Benjamin, when justice was denied them against the abusers of the Levite's concubine Jehu. None of the kings of Israel, whether good or bad, had any title other than as conferred to them by the people. The people could not have given them any power unless they had it themselves, for which they needed to meet and consent, even if it was against the will of those who reigned.

¶ **107.** The Kingdom of Edom appointed a deputy instead of a king to rule over them, since there was no king in Edom. It should be obvious by now that their **kings and governors are chosen by the people**. Decisions such as who can reign and who cannot are made by nations, provided said nations act for good reasons and are moved by just causes. As such, these are not only allowed but approved by God, the Lover of Justice, who **always intends the welfare and happiness of mankind**.

¶ **108. If the subject may not resist, then there is no law, only the will and pleasure of the prince. If one can be opposed in nothing, he may do everything. Then, all our laws lose meaning, which makes the law-makers fools or madmen who give themselves trouble to no purpose. If the king is not obliged to govern by the laws they make, why would the people obey them?**

¶ **109.** If the king would sue me by pretence of law and endeavour to take away my money, my house or my land, I may defend them by the Law. But if he comes armed to take away our Liberty, Life or Religion, which are ours by the Laws of God and Man, may we not secure them in good conscience?

¶ 110. Every man has a right to preserve himself, his liberties, and privileges against anyone, because no one has authority to invade them. This was the case of Sampson who went to war against the Philistines for burning his wife and her father. Sampson was but **a private man**, who knew he **could have no other kind of justice against them than what the Law of Nature gives every man.**

¶ 111. The work of all magistrates everywhere is always the same: ensuring that justice is done and ensuring the welfare of those who elevated them. This is common sense. Plato, Aristotle, Cicero and the best authors lay it as an immoveable foundation, on which they build their arguments relating to matters of that nature.

The Apostle Paul declared in *Romans* XIII *That* **Rulers are not a Terror to good Works, but to evil.** *Will you not then be afraid of the Power? Do what is good, and you shall have Praise for* **being the Minister of God for good**; *but if you do that which is evil, be afraid; for he bears not the Sword in vain who is the Minister of God, a Revenger on the evil doers.*

St. Paul gives a reason for praying for kings and all in authority *That we may live a quiet and peaceable Life, in all Godliness and Honesty.*

The tables are turned, and the institution vacated if the praise is aimed at evil doers who terrorise those who do good. Then the honest and just people cannot stay quiet. If God be the fountain of Justice, Mercy, and Truth and the people who live by them His servants, they would not patronise violence, fraud, cruelty, pride or avarice. The authors of such crimes can only be the minions of all who set themselves against God, because it is impossible that truth and falsehood, mercy and cruelty, justice and oppression can proceed from the same root.

The Jews who called themselves Children of Abraham but did not do Abraham's work were liars and Christ declared them to be Children of the Devil, doing his work, *John* VIII 39, 44.

All princes, therefore, cannot be equally ministers of God. Their actions manifest the truth. They should use their power to encourage virtue and discourage vice. **The same rule which obliges us to yield obedience to the good magistrate, a minister of God, does equally oblige us not to obey the bad magistrates, the ministers of the Devil.**

The Apostle commands us to obey the ministers of God for our own good, **but not to obey the ministers of the devil, for we cannot serve two masters.**

¶ 112. St. Chrysostom interpreted the words of St. Paul in the following way: every soul is subject to a higher power. Yet it was never the intention to overthrow governments or the constitutions of nations **in order to subject all to one man's will. Every good emperor in history has acknowledged that the Laws of his empire are above him.** This principle of government was adopted by all civilized nations.

According to Pindar, Herodotus calls **the Law, King over all.** In his Hymns, Orpheus calls it *the King of Gods and Men.* Plato, in his *Epistles*[44], promotes the form of government in which **the Law is made Lord and Master, and no scope is given to any man to step over the Laws.**

Aristotle is of the same opinion in his *Politics.* Cicero, in his book *De Legibus*[45], declares that "**the Laws ought to govern the Magistrate, as they do the People**". The Law, therefore, in the opinion of the wisest and most learned men in history, and by the constitution, has always been the highest power on earth. It is very clear that the doctrine of the Gospel contradicts neither reason, nor the laws of the nations. Man is

---

[44] From Greek: letters, messages, commands
[45] Latin: *Of the Laws*

truly and properly subject to the highest power, which is the Law, and the magistrates must govern according to Law.

St. Paul did not only command the people but the princes themselves to respect the laws and remain bound by them, *"For there is no Power but of God"*. The most ancient Laws that are known to us were credited to God as their author. *"**The Law**"*, says Cicero in his *Politics*, "**is but a rule of well-grounded Reason, derived from God himself, enjoying whatever is just and right, and forbidding the contrary.**"

¶ 113. I challenge any man to produce evidence from Scripture that allows absolute authority to governors, magistrates, kings, or princes. Where there is no absolute authority, there can be no absolute obedience.

¶ 114. During the reign of Darius, the laws were made by the people. This was true to such an extent that, since the king was subject to the laws, he had no power to suspend the execution of Daniel, his favourite, considered the greatest man in the kingdom after the king. The king made a huge effort to save the Prophet, yet the law prevailed, and Darius could not save him. So, Daniel was thrown to the lions, proving **the superiority of the Law over kingly power**. As powerful as Darius was, he bowed to the regency of the law and acknowledged he was unable to alter it. Undoubtedly, the limitation of power and the superiority of the laws in all matters of government originate in antiquity.

¶ 115. The doctrine of absolute passive obedience is inconsistent with the goodness of God and the love He has for man. It destroys the purpose, intent, and design of God's Laws, which are made to ensure man's happiness.

For God, who is infinitely happy, the only motivation for creating rules for man to follow is man's happiness. It is why he made it a duty to help the poor and miserable, to relieve the oppressed and distressed and to be kind and good to one another. Can it then be presumed that God would require obedience to a tyrannical power, which brings poverty, misery, and desolation to the people? If it is a duty to relieve the poor, it must be a duty to prevent people falling into misery by **having the right to oppose arbitrary power. And if it is a duty to promote the public good, then it must be a duty to oppose tyrannical government**.

¶ **116.** **The promoting of passive obedience is a much greater crime than the encouraging of rebellion**, because a civil war, although painful, cannot continue long, and a nation may flourish and be happy again. But if **arbitrary government is introduced on the principles of passive obedience, people's miseries are endless and there is no hope of redress**.

Every age will then add new cruelties and burdens to a people already exhausted. Those who preach and promote absolute passive obedience do not understand that it removes all protections designed to safeguard not only the people's lands, but also their liberties and lives, and prostrates them at the feet of a single person.

Our ancestors were utterly unacquainted with this doctrine, which can never be entertained by free-born subjects, nor has it any other use than to encourage kings to become tyrants. All ages before us can attest to the fatal confluences, which always attend tyranny, and the dreadful effects of arbitrary power.

¶ **117.** It is just a few priests of the Church of England who preach the doctrine of absolute obedience and non-resistance as necessary to our salvation, and yet its origins cannot be found in scripture or in known history. How is it possible that it doesn't cross their minds to compare their hypothesis to the opinions of learned men before us? They are shameless and blind to the terrible consequences of this doctrine on our kingdom.

¶ **118.** It is a wonder how freedom-loving men would maintain maxims so pernicious to humane society. If this doctrine had gained traction, we and all of Europe would be miserably toiling under tyranny and oppression to this day. A king needs no army to ruin and enslave his people; with a few mean slaves, he could rob them of their lives and fortunes.

¶ **119. The greatest and wisest of men in all ages and nations have considered it perfectly lawful for the people to do justice themselves in case of oppression. They have thought it an unavoidable duty and one which they owed to their posterity.** The chief instruments of the great revolutions in the world, the changes from slavery to liberty, have always been accounted as heroes, sent by God Almighty for the redemption of man from misery in this world. These heroes were honoured and respected whilst they lived, and their memories have been and will be held in veneration by all future generations.

¶ **120. The doctrine of absolute passive obedience is a treasonable, enslaving, and pernicious doctrine, which takes away people's civil rights, their self-defence mechanism, which is the Law of God and Nature, and supplies the king's government with absolute authority.** If all the revolutions and replacements of kings in England are made out as damnable rebellions and usurpations, then all our kings and queens would be usurpers and the Stuarts would be deemed usurpers, regardless of being the lawful issue of Henry VII, who was made king by virtue of an Act of Parliament. It would make the Glorious Revolution a damnable rebellion and usurpation, and the Queen herself a rebel and usurper. This doctrine is truly detestable.

¶ **121.** What do you have to say for yourselves now, all of you patrons and preachers of this enslaving doctrine? You deserve that a Bill of Indictment for High Treason be made against you for denying the power of the people, who made changes of government. The people made and confirmed the last Revolution in all the succeeding parliaments. This Revolution King, with the Lords and Commons in Parliament assembled, who altered the succession from the House of Savoy to the House of Hanover, was the entire legislative authority of the nation! Deny this if you dare. This is another example of ***Vox Populi***.

¶ **122. The doctrine of absolute passive obedience is a treasonable doctrine against civil society** because it encourages tyranny. Let us suppose that one of our generals should suggest to his soldiers that the government was not managed well, or that justice and equity are not truly performed. Let us say that, by promises of money and preferential treatment to the officers and soldiers, he got on the throne with their assistance. But when on the throne, he acted as God's Vicegerent[46] and was not to be resisted upon pain of damnation, according to the doctrine of absolute passive obedience. So, if a tyrant or usurper should get on the throne, the people must be passive as they have no power, only the magistrate. Although the people have power and authority to choose this magistrate, the very minute he is chosen, their power and authority vanishes, and, if he should turn into a tyrant, they have nothing but prayers and tears to help them.

If that were the case, the laws don't matter, as the magistrate's will and pleasure are placed above them, even if he proves to be a terror to good and a rewarder of evil, acting diametrically contrary to the nature and design of his office. He could rob, burn, and destroy all before him but because he is still God's Vicegerent, he is not to be resisted.

---

[46] Biblical connotation: one chosen to represent God on Earth (eg. the Pope); an administrative deputy, a surrogate.

Who would dare challenge him? Do you realise now, you enemies to church and state, that you should stop teaching the doctrine of absolute passive obedience?

¶ **123.** The doctrine of passive obedience failed when the Lords Spiritual and Temporal, the gentlemen, and commonalty invited the Prince of Orange to come with armed forces to compel the God's Vicegerent (King James), their prior lawful sovereign, to revoke his wrongdoings and to bind him in chains, together with his nobles. He failed to govern according to Law, imposing his will and pleasure on the people. The nobility, gentry, and commonalty spontaneously rose to join the Prince of Orange. The bishops and noblemen met at Guildhall and asked the prince to accept the administration of the government. The Convention of the Lords Spiritual and Temporal gave the crown and dignity to the Prince and Princess of Orange, while parliament waged war against King James in Ireland.

¶ **124.** On the 3rd of October 1688, the Archbishop of Canterbury, the bishops of London, Winchester, Asaph, Ely, Chichester, Rochester, Bath and Wells, and Peterborough, all in person, listened to the speech the Archbishop made to the king. Afterwards, the Archbishop read and delivered to him ten articles for the redress of the abuses in government, the substance of which was very near the same to that of the Prince of Orange's declaration. The articles were drawn at Lambeth on the 1st of October, the very same day that the prince's declaration was signed in Holland.

¶ **125.** On the 1st of November 1688, a parcel of the Prince of Orange's declarations was intercepted in London. The prince was invited to England by various Lords, both Spiritual and Temporal, as well as others. King James summoned some of the bishops again and required them to sign a paper (Abhorrence) rejecting the Prince of Orange's intended invasion. This paper was designed to be part of a proclamation due to be published in order to suppress the prince's declaration.

The bishops of Canterbury, London, Peterborough, and Rochester refused to do it, upon which his Majesty was very much incensed by them. The Bishop of Rochester said this on the matter: *"...the Jesuited[47] Party at Court were so violently enraged, that as we are credibly informed ..., they should all be imprisoned and the Truth extorted from them ..."*.

¶ **126.**   The doctrine of passive obedience failed again on the 5th of November 1688, when the Prince of Orange landed. On the 12th, the royal Regiment of Dragoons and the Duke of St. Alban's Regiment of Horse joined the prince.

On the 15th of November, the prince addressed the gentry of Somersetshire and Dorsetshire at Exeter, saying: *"Although we do not know all of you, we are aware of your names and the strength of your character and passion for your country. We come on your invitation and by our promise. Our duty to God obliges us to protect the protestant religion, and our love of mankind, your liberties and properties"*. In conclusion, the prince vowed: *"Let the world now judge if our aspirations are not just, generous and sincere, since even though we have a Bridge of Gold to return to, it is our principled resolution that we rather die in a good cause than live in a bad one, well knowing that virtue and true honour is its own reward and the happiness of mankind our great and only design."*

On the 16th, the Lord Delamere assembled fifty horsemen and marched to Manchester, then to Boden-Downs. When his forces increased to one hundred and fifty, he declared his plan to join the Prince of Orange and this small party gradually drew in the Earls of Devonshire, Stamford, Danby, and all the North.

---

[47] In its original biblical meaning, a Jesuit was someone who invoked the name of Jesus way too frequently for no good reason.

¶ **127.** The doctrine of absolute passive obedience and unconditional loyalty failed yet again when Sancroft, Archbishop of Canterbury, who was the first to sign the Prince of Orange's Invitation to the City, demanded the keys of the tower from King James's lieutenant, Sir Bevel Skelton, in the name of the Lord Mayor. The Lords Spiritual and Temporal then assembled at Guildhall and the lieutenant surrendered to them the keys, as King James had forfeited the duty and obedience of his subjects.

¶ **128.** The doctrine failed when Prince George of Denmark, the Duke of Grafton, Duke of Ormond, and many others of the protestant nobility went over to the Prince of Orange at Sherborn Castle. On the 29th of November, Bristol was seized by the Earl of Shrewsbury and Sir John Guise. The gentry of Gloucestershire freed Lord Lovelace from the Castle of Gloucester, where he was a prisoner. Newcastle and York were in the hands of the allied Lords, while the garrison of Hull seized Langdale, their papist governor, and disarmed the newly sent popish forces.

¶ **129.** On the 4th of December, Prince George of Denmark, the Duke of Ormond, Lord Mordant, Earl of Macclesfield, and several other lords, as well as many knights and gentlemen, rode into the city of Salisbury with the Prince of Orange and his army. The Princess Ann, our most gracious and good queen, accompanied by the Lady Churchill, now Duchess of Marlborough, Lady Berkley, and the Bishop of London, went to the North to join the forces in arms for the Prince of Orange.

On the 5th of December, the Earl of Oxford joined the Prince of Orange at Salisbury. The same day, Sir Edward Hurley and most of the gentry of Worcestershire and Herefordshire met at Worcester and declared for the Prince of Orange. Ludlow Castle was taken for the prince by the Lord Herbert and Sir Walter Blount, and the popish Sheriff of Worcester was secured in it.

On the 11th of December, about three in the morning, the bad king went to Gravesend in a small boat. At about ten o'clock, the Lords Spiritual and Temporal, who were in the vicinity, came to Guildhall in London and sent for the Lord Mayor and the Aldermen. They made the following Declaration:

There is no doubt that in these dangerous times we are wholeheartedly concerned for the protestant religion, the Laws of the Land, and the Liberties and Properties of the Subjects. His Majesty has withdrawn himself. We, therefore, unanimously resolve to apply ourselves to his Highness the Prince of Orange.

And we do hereby declare that we will unreservedly assist his Highness to obtain with all speed such a parliament, wherein our Laws, Liberties and Properties may be secured, particularly the Church of England, with a due Liberty to protestant dissenters. In general, we support and encourage the protestant religion and interest over the whole world to the Glory of God, the happiness of the established government in all kingdoms and the advantage of all princes and states in Christendom. In the meantime, we will endeavour as much as we can to preserve the peace and security of these great and populous cities of London and Westminster, as well as their adjacent parts, by taking care to disarm all papists and secure all Jesuits and Roman priests therein. And if there is anything more we can do to promote his Highness's generous intentions for the public good, we stand ready to do it as the occasion requires.

Signed by W. Cant, T. Ebor, Pembrook, Dorset, Mulgrave, Thanet, Carlisle, Craven, Aylesbury, Burlington, Sussex, Berkeley, Rochester, Newport, Weymouth, P. Winchester, W. Asaph, F. Ely, Tho. Rossen, Tho. Petriburg, P. Wharton, North and Gray, Chandris, Montague, T. Jermyn, Vaughan, Carbery, Culpepper, Crew, Osulston.

The Earl of Pembrook, the Lord Viscount Weymouth, the Bishop of Ely, and the Lord Culpepper were ordered to present this declaration to his Highness, the Prince of Orange.

The declaration was dated at Guildhall, the 11th of December 1688, in opposition to the doctrine of absolute passive obedience to tyranny.

¶ **130.** The same day, at Guildhall, the lieutenancy of London signed the following address to the Prince of Orange and sent it by Sir Robert Clayton, Sir William Russell, Sir Bazil Firebrace, and Charles Duncomb, Esquire:

May it please your Highness,

We can never sufficiently express our deep and eternal gratitude for your Highness exposing yourself to numerous dangers by sea and land for the preservation of the protestant religion and the Laws and Liberties of this Kingdom. Without your unparalleled bravery, we would probably have suffered all the miseries of popery and slavery. We were greatly concerned that prior to this, we had no opportunity to assure your Highness that it has been our firm resolution to risk all that is dear to us to achieve the glorious goals your Highness has proposed for restoring this distracted nation. We therefore now unanimously present to your Highness our acknowledgements for the happy relief you have brought us. We also assure you that we have positioned ourselves so that by the blessing of God we may be able to prevent all evil plans and preserve this city in peace and safety. We know your Highness will repair this city with what convenient speed you can, thus perfecting the great work your Highness has so happily begun to the joy and satisfaction of us all.

¶ **131.** On the same day, the 11th of December 1688, the Lord Mayor, the aldermen, and the commons of the city of London assembled in common council, and agreed and signed an address to the Prince of Orange, imploring his protection and humbly beseeching him to repair the city, where his Highness would be received with universal joy and satisfaction.

On the 14th of December, at Henley upon Thames, all addresses were presented to his Highness, the Prince of Orange, by the persons appointed, quite contrary to the doctrine of unconditional obedience of Dr. Hicks, Dr. Whelton, Dr. Atterbury, Dr. Sacheverell, etc.

¶ **132.** On the 14th of December, the Privy Council and the peers met again at the council chamber at Whitehall and issued an order requiring all Irish officers and soldiers to surrender their arms, which were to be deposited in the tower of London.

¶ **133.** By that time, all the forts in England, except Portsmouth and Tilbury, were in the prince's control. By order of the Lords of the Council, the Duke of Grafton marched through the Strand at the head of a foot regiment of guards to take Tilbury out of the hands of King James's Irish soldiers.

On the 18th, the king went to Rochester, while the Prince of Orange came to St. James's, attended by a great number of nobility and gentry.

On the 20th, the councilmen and aldermen went to St. James's, where Sir George Treby, their recorder, made the following speech on their behalf:

¶ 134.

May it please your Highness,

As the Lord Mayor is disabled by sickness, the aldermen and commons of the capital city of this kingdom are deputed to congratulate your Highness on this great and glorious occasion.

We are short of words when we think of the recent danger, our church and state overrun by papal influence and arbitrary power, brought to the point of destruction by the conduct of men who broke our sacred Laws and the very constitution of our legislature.

Your Highness was our last remedy as you are the only person to help us. You are of an agreeable allied nation. You are a sovereign prince of a most illustrious family, benefactors of mankind, who have long been champions of Almighty God, vindicating His Cause against the greatest oppressions in history.

Our nobles, our gentry and our brave English soldiers render themselves and their arms at your command.

Great Sir,

When we look back to the last month and contemplate the speed of our present deliverance, it seems miraculous.

Your Highness, led by the Hand of Heaven and called by the Voice of the People, has preserved our dearest interests: the protestant religion, which is primitive Christianity, and our Laws, which are our ancient title to our lives, liberties and estates, and without which, this world would be a wilderness.

How can we repay your Highness? We are deeply grateful.

Your Highness has a lasting monument in the hearts and in the prayers and praises of all good men among us.

And late posterity will celebrate your ever glorious name, till time shall be no more.

¶ **135.** On the 21st of December 1688, about sixty of the peers met at St. James's and signed a paper in the nature of an association. His Highness then gave them a short speech.

¶ **136.** On the 22nd of December, the Lords Spiritual and Temporal assembled in the House of Lords at Westminster and appointed Francis Gwyn to sign their orders.

¶ **137.** On the 23rd of December, King James went to Dover and sailed for France.

¶ **138.** The above-mentioned peers assembled on the 25th of December in the House of Lords and signed and presented to his Highness the following address:

We, the Lords Spiritual and Temporal assembled in this Conjuncture, do desire your Highness to take upon you the Administration of the Public Affairs, both Civil and Military, and the Disposal of the Public Revenue, for the Preservation of our Religion, Rights, Laws, Liberties and Properties, and of the Peace of the Nation, till the meeting of the Convention, January 22nd.

The lords humbly asked his Highness to sign the letters to all the protestant lords and all the counties, inviting them to send members to the Convention on the 22nd of January 1689.

¶ **139.** On the 19th of January, about thirty lords and eighty gentlemen of Scotland signed a similar paper, which was delivered to his Highness by the Duke of Hamilton, their president.

¶ **140.**

On the 22nd of January 1689, the Convention met and ordered *that both Houses return thanks to his Highness on behalf of the nation for his deliverance of the kingdom from popery, slavery, and despotic power, and for the preservation of the protestant religion and the Laws, Rights, Privileges, and Customs of our Land.* Both Houses ordered a day of public thanksgiving in London and Westminster, and within ten miles radius, on the 31st of January. Later, it was extended to the whole kingdom.

¶ **141.** On the 28th of January, the Convention resolved that *King James II, who subverted the Constitution of this kingdom by breaking the original contract between King and People, following the advice of Jesuits and other wicked persons, and violated the fundamental Laws. Having withdrawn himself from this kingdom, he has abdicated the government, and the throne has thereby become vacant.*

¶ **142.** The word "abdicated"[48] relates to all of the above and to deserting the kingdom. It means that King James, by violating the original contract and by endeavouring to subvert the constitution, **did** ***abdicate*** the government. That is, by refusing to govern us according to the same Law by which he held the Crown, he implicitly renounced his title to it. **It is an undeniable right, inherent and inseparable from all nations, to have the same power of making laws for their own preservation and government that their ancestors had.**

¶ **143.** On the 12th of February 1689, the Lords Spiritual and Temporal and the Commons declared William and Mary formerly of Orange, King and Queen of England.

¶ **144.** A proclamation of the Lords and Commons was then published:

The Prince and Princess of Orange accepted the Crown according to their desire: we, therefore, the Lords Spiritual and Temporal, and Commons, together with the Lord Mayor and citizens of London, and others of the commons of this realm, with full consent publish and proclaim William and Mary, Prince and Princess of Orange, to be King and Queen of England.

---

[48] From Latin *ab* [off, away] and *dicare* [speak, declare]

None of this was according to the doctrine of absolute passive obedience. By this revolution the body of the people of England are restored to their ancient right and the government re-established upon its primitive and original foundation. The pretended divine right of succession has now vanished.

¶ **145.** The Nottingham declaration of the nobility, gentry and commonalty assembled to assist the Prince of Orange says: *We hope all good protestant subjects will assist us with their lives and fortunes and will not be deterred by the scornful smears aimed to frighten us into becoming slaves to tyrannical usurpations. No rational and unbiased person will judge it rebellion to defend our laws and religion, to which all our princes have sworn at their Coronation. Rebellion is to resist a king that governs by Law; yet a king was always considered a tyrant if he made his will the law. To resist such a king is no rebellion, but a necessary defence, and we do not doubt all honest men's assistance and implore God's protection. People can never be of one mind without God's inspiration and in all ages, it has been confirmed that* **Vox Populi est Vox Dei.**

¶ **146.** There were bishops, clergy, nobility, and commonalty, who kept preaching the doctrine of passive obedience during the Revolution. St Paul's damnation be on them.

¶ **147.** This ridiculous doctrine of Kings being *Jure Divino* (divine law) was first preached In King James I's reign. It was never heard of before, but the doctrine of passive obedience without reserve took purchase in King Charles I's time, when Popish and French councils were allowed at court. There is no proof at all of divine appointment of kings or of any other governors, so as to be a rule for any people or nation to go by. If it were true, that would make God the author or approver of all tyranny, thievery, murder, and desolation in the world, which is a damnable sin to assert.

¶ 148. This nonsensical enslaving doctrine of passive obedience to tyranny had no place when the children of Israel slew Amaziah, their lawful king, for his idolatry. And yet, no one ever called this "rebellion", nor were they punished by his son, Uzziah, who was made king in his father's stead.

Saul's subjects swore that Saul should not kill Jonathan and they saved him from dying, *Samuel* XIV 45. Although the people sinned grievously in asking for a king, God assented to their demand. No prince was ever more solemnly instituted than Saul. The people chose him by lot from amongst all the tribes, and he was placed in the throne by the general consent of the whole nation. But he turned his lawful power into tyranny, disobeyed the word of the Prophet, slayed the priests, and oppressed the innocent, thus overthrowing his own right. God declared the kingdom, which had been given to Saul, to be entirely abrogated.

This gave the people as a whole, and every man in particular, the right to oppose him. David contained his fury and led all the discontented people who would follow him. He kept them in arms against Saul and lived in the country. He was betrayed by Nabash who refused to send provisions for his men and, finding himself weak and unsafe, went to Achish the Philistine and offered his service against Israel.

This was never regarded as a sin in David, except by the wicked court-flatterer Doeg the Edomite and the drunken fool Nabal, who is said to be a man of Belial. By arming as many as came to him, David sufficiently showed his intention to resist rather than to run.

David had no other right to go to war against Saul or Ishbosheth, Saul's son, save that the tribe of Judaea had made him king. Although designed by God and anointed by the Prophet, David resisted the authority of Ishbosheth without assuming the power of a king until he was made king of Judaea. That is how he entered into a covenant with the Judean people. If Saul, who was made king by the whole people and anointed by the command of God, might be resisted when he departed from the Law of his institution, there is no doubt that any other may be resisted for the like reason. If resistance was unlawful and a sin, surely David, a man after God's own heart, would have known it and would not have involved the six hundred men that came to his assistance in "the sin of rebellion". According to the pretended doctrine of divine right, any slave in Israel would have become the Lord's anointed if he killed David or Solomon and put a villain on the throne to replace them.

¶ **149.** There was no doctrine of absolute passive obedience when the primitive Christians called on Constantine the Great to aid and assist them with force of arms against the tyranny and persecution of Maxentius and Maximinius, nor when the primitive Christians, with Constantine's help, resisted their emperor Lucinius for persecuting them contrary to Law. Eusebius described Constantine the Great as one "*who held it his duty to save an infinite number of people by cutting off a few wicked ones*".

The primitive Christians under the king of Persia resisted him for his persecutions with the help of the Roman Emperor Theodosius. The Christians of Armenia allied themselves with the Romans to secure their lives and religion against the Persians, under whom they lived.

The Novatians, assisted by the Orthodox, resisted and beat the Macedonians. The primitive Christians then destroyed Julian's idolatrous temple. The Lutheran Churches defended themselves against the emperor Charles V. The Protestants of Austria took up arms in 1608 against Matthias, king of Hungary, for denying them the free exercise of their religion.

¶ **150.** The cruel and barbarous doctrine of absolute passive obedience failed when the whole Church of England justified the protestants in resisting their tyrannical princes. The Church did so not just in words but helped financially by charging itself deeply with taxes. The evidence is in the Clergy's Subsidy Acts in the reign of Queen Elizabeth[49].

---

[49] Elizabeth I inherited the most debased coinage in the history of the monarchy. Within a year she restored trust in the English coin by melting the debased money and replacing it with newly minted precious metal coins, earning herself a tidy profit. The Subsidies of the Clergy (1597) represented the grants by the

¶ **151.** Among other considerations for which the clergy gave their subsidy of six shillings in the pound were *"the inestimable charges sustained by her Highness"* for *"the abating of all hostility and persecution against the professors of God's holy Gospel and true religion".*

The Queen assisted the Scottish in their Reformation, even though they were opposed by the Queen of Scots. The Temporality[50], in their Subsidy Act, called this assistance "rightful preservation" of the Liberty of the nation of Scotland from eminent captivity and desolation.

This assistance of the Queen, parliament, and clergy would have been a damnable sin, according to the doctrine of absolute passive and unconditional obedience, which some of our clergy now hold. Yet all the bishops and clergy in convocation held no such doctrine. They called it use of "godly and prudent means to abate hostility and persecution" against the proponents of the Gospel and true religion.

¶ **152.** The clergy granted an additional subsidy for Her Majesty's expenses, "in the provident and needful prevention of the extirpation of the sincere profession of the Gospel, both here and elsewhere".

The Parliament's Subsidy Act at the same time declared the following reasons for their tax: *Your Majesty has become the principal support of just and religious causes against usurpers. In addition to the great help in France and Flanders, this land has become a haven of refuge for states and kingdoms, and a rock and bulwark of opposition against tyrannical and usurping rulers.*

¶ **153.** The clergy's Subsidy Act says: *Anyone with common sense would remember your Majesty's courage and persistence in protecting the free profession of the Gospel, within and without your Majesty's dominions.*

---

clergy to Queen Elizabeth, which were levied twice a year over a three-year period (initially) at 2 shillings to the pound.

[50] I.e. the spiritual or ecclesiastical power or authority.

King Charles I and the bishops and clergy of England assisted the protestants of France, as well as the Scottish and Dutch protestants. Without the help of the Church and Parliament of England, they would have been doomed rebels in the resistance against their lawful sovereigns, **because it is utterly unlawful and a horrid sin to assist subjects in the violation of their duty and allegiance, and to aid them in resisting the ordinance of God**.

This, however, is too absurd to be believed by anyone who had risked their life for the protestant religion. If it was unlawful to assist subjects against tyrannical princes, then those protectors have been willing to pay a very dear price, since they applied a whole year's revenue of all the benefices of England to their cause. **It appears that the new fashionable doctrine of submitting to all sorts of lawless oppression is madness and wholly unknown to the compilers of our *Homilies*.**

¶ **154.** The protestant princes of Germany didn't practice absolute passive obedience but invited Gustavus Adolphus, King of Sweden, to assist them against their own prince for persecuting them.

¶ **155.** Bishop Jewel wrote in his *Apology*: **no one ever taught the people to rebel against their prince, but only to defend themselves by all lawful means against oppression, as did David against King Saul.**

So do the nobles in France nowadays: they seek to save their lives by protesting through writing to the world. They are best acquainted with the laws and constitution of their country and, therefore, best able to account for the grounds and reasons of their actions.

¶ **156.** Bishop Bilson, in his book on the *Difference between Christian Subjection and Unchristian Rebellion* (dedicated to Queen Elizabeth), wrote in defence of the French, who protested the unjust oppressions of their king, *"I will not rashly pronounce all who resist to be rebels: cases may fall out in Christian Kingdoms where people may plead their right against the prince and not be charged with rebellion"*. As an example, he points to situations where a prince subjects his kingdom to a foreign realm or changes the form of the commonwealth from empire to tyranny, or neglects the laws established by common consent of the people or acts to satisfy his own pleasure. The nobles and commons are not rebels if they join forces and rise to defend their ancient and accustomed Liberty.

¶ **157.** In King Charles I's reign, Bishop Abbot commented on the difference between the primitive Christians and us, saying, that while they had no legal right for their religion, they were subject to the "pleasure" of the government. This changed when they fell under emperor Constantine, as they had laws on their side and their resistance became lawful.

¶ **158.** Luther[51] had always taught that the magistrate should not be resisted. However, when the lawyers got together in a conference and proved that *"resistance was allowed by the Laws in some cases"*, Luther cleverly responded that he didn't know this before. Then he said, ***"The Gospel does not bar, nor abolish the Laws of the State"***, and that ***"Not only a matter of right, but also the force and necessity of conscience might force us to arms"***.

¶ **159.**

At the same time, there were seven princes and twenty-four protestant cities, which entered an alliance against the emperor. They declared this: *As for his charging us with rebellion, there is nothing at all in it and he knows in his*

---

[51] Martin Luther (1483-1546), a German monk credited with initiating the Protestant Reformation.

conscience that we are wronged. **If he had complied with his contract and decrees, we would have done our duty. But because he has broken them, let him lay the blame upon himself. Since he endeavours the destruction of our religion and Liberty, he gives us cause to oppose him in good conscience. Unjust violence is by no means the Ordinance of God and he ceased the performance of the conditions on which he was made emperor.**

¶ **160.** The citizens of Magdeburgh could not be proved guilty of rebellion either by the Law of God or the Law of Man: *Those who took up arms against the people made war upon Christ himself. It is utterly unlawful to offer any violence to us.*

¶ **161.** Melanchthon was of the same opinion as Luther regarding the lawfulness of resistance, as was St. Chrysostom before them both. In his commentary on *Proverbs* XXIV 21- 22, he said: *The Gospel allows us to make use of political laws, which are* **reasonable**.

And in *Vindicta*, we read these words of our Saviour, "**He that takes the Sword, shall perish by the Sword**". And further: "**For a Man to take the Sword, is to draw it when it is not put into his hands by the Laws. Therefore, he who offers unjust violence, takes the sword. But on the other hand, he who uses a just defence draws the Sword put into his hands by the Laws**".

In his commentary on *Romans* XIII, we read that one must be a subject not only for "wrath", but also for "conscience". He also says, "**These words concern not only the subject but also the magistrates themselves who, when they turn tyrants, overthrow the Ordinance of God, no less than the seditious**". And finally, "**Let no person think the violation of the Constitution to be a light sin!**"

¶ **162.** Zuinglius, one of the first Swiss reformers, affirms that *Those who live under oppression, deserve what they suffer. No wrong is done to them.* He articulately explains that if the people accept unjust punishments inflicted by a magistrate without opposing him, then they deserve their fate.

¶ **163.** Lucifer de Cagliari in his book *De non parciendo in delinquentibus*[52] declares, "*It was lawful to resist kings under the Old Testament, and also to put them to death in case of idolatry.*"

¶ **164.** St. Austin commented on the behaviour of the Christians towards emperor Julian in this way: *The Christian soldiers served under this infidel emperor, and where their religion was not concerned, made conscience of obeying him; but where it came to the cause of Christ, there they made as much conscience of disobeying him.*"

¶ **165.** In the beginning of the Reformation, the European protestants fell under oppression. All of them, including the French, Scottish, and Dutch protestants, defended themselves by resistance. In Scotland, this ended in an established Reformation of the protestant religion; in Holland, it ended in an absolute freedom; and in France, it ended in a free exercise of their religion, which was too soon interrupted by the popish massacre and the French were forced to fight all over again against the same tyranny and oppression.

Neither of them ever pretended that their religion was established by law and, hence, a part of the government of their country, which men were bound to defend. Still, they repelled the violence against their civil rights and the innate Liberty of their consciences.

---

[52] Latin: *On not sparing the criminals.*

¶ **166.** The government of the Roman emperors was absolute and straightforward. They governed at their pleasure, made and unmade laws to serve them, and had the sovereign power of life and death. For this reason, the Christians could resist the violence of those times, as well as defend themselves against the wrongs done to them. While this continued, the Christians were killed, but did not kill. Regardless, when under the emperor Constantine, they opted for killing rather than being killed. Having vanquished several usurpers, they threw off the yoke of persecution.

¶ **167.** If God had commanded the subjection to the will and pleasure of princes, isn't it strange that neither of the Prophets, nor the Jews, or the primitive Christians, or any of the ancient fathers, or the reformed churches ever knew of this doctrine of absolute passive obedience to the will of tyrannical princes?

¶ **168.**

If resisting the supreme authority were unlawful in any circumstance, why have so many people acted "in rebellion" throughout all of history, throwing out their destructive kings and governors? The Christians in all ages have done so and were justified. Only the supporters of the doctrine of passive obedience consider it rebellious to act against tyranny.

¶ **169. It is unjust and unreasonable to assert any absolute passive obedience but to the Laws of God and the Laws of the Land.** For any of our nobility or gentry etc., who had a hand in the late Revolution, to suffer preachings of passive obedience by members of either House of the Convention Parliament is to suffer themselves to be called rebels and traitors, and the Revolution a damned rebellion.

¶ **170.** **He that lets any person destroy him contrary to law, when it is in his power to preserve his life by defending himself, tacitly consents to his own death. By the Laws of Nature, he is obliged to defend his life and, therefore is guilty of his own destruction.** Whereas by defending himself, only the attacker can be guilty of spilling blood. It then follows that **passive obedience to unjust violence is a sin, yet resisting such violence is no sin, but rather the duty of every man.** The first duty I owe is to God, the second is for my self-preservation, and the third is to my parent and sovereign to obey him in all things reasonable and lawful.

¶ **171.** **The doctrine of passive obedience without reserve is diametrically opposite to the law of self-preservation, which is simultaneously the Law of Nature and the decree of the Almighty. This is a sacred Law, not to be infringed by any man.**

¶ **172.** It is not the doctrine of the Gospel, or of Jesus Christ, to be passive beyond the laws and customs of the country. That would make God the author or approver of all persecutions and innocent spilling of blood by evil princes and governors. God never commanded anything contrary to the Law of Nature.

¶ **173.** **All men have a natural and a civil right and property in their lives** until they have forfeited them by the laws of their country.

¶ **174.** When the law of a country makes it a capital crime to be Christian, then the people are to lay down their lives for Christ's sake. Only then would the Gospel require passive obedience, when the laws are against man, as was the case with the first Christians.

¶ **175.** The Gospel is so far from enslaving us or divesting us of rights and privileges, that it encourages us to procure more liberties and franchises, if we can come honestly by them.

¶ **176.** St. Paul was not preaching absolute passive obedience in his hour of need. When the chief captain commanded that he be whipped, he said to the Centurion, *"Is it lawful for you to scourge a Roman uncondemned?"*. He and Silas were accused and found guilty of breaking the Roman laws by teaching customs which were not lawful at the time. The magistrates of Philippi, one of the chief cities of Macedonia, had put them in prison and beaten them for it, and would have let them go, but St. Paul contested that they were beaten illegally and would not leave prison. Eventually, the magistrates got them out.

¶ **177.** According to Paul's plea to the Romans, all magistrates are the powers that be, but not the supreme powers that be. *"The powers that be were ordained of God"* implies that all magistrates are with those powers. According to St. Paul, then, the Lord Mayor and all the aldermen of London (except those few who are not Justices of the Peace), as well as all constables are with such powers. Those powers were chosen: ***Vox Populi, Vox Dei***. To resist any of these powers in the administration or execution of the laws is a sin, and every sin in its nature is damnable.

Yet these powers may be resisted, prosecuted, and punished, according to the nature of the crimes committed with them. The magistrates are not ordained of God, nor have their power from God, any more than all men are ordained of God and have their lives from him. This is their power and in the execution of it, they have power to do good or evil. Before they are chosen magistrates, they have no more power than other men, but when chosen, the Law is their power, beyond which they cannot go without incurring a penalty.

¶ **178.** According to our Constitution, the powers are **the legislative authority of this nation,** vested in the three estates in Parliament Assembled, who are the supreme powers with ability to make or annihilate laws. These powers are as much the Ordinance of God as any other power. To resist these powers in making or unmaking laws is a damnable sin. However, when these persons are separated from their authority, they are but private persons, who have no more power than any other person and are punishable by the laws of their own making, just like any other person. The main power is that of the king, because in him is the executive part of these powers, which is executing the powers of the laws. All persons commissioned by him, such as the Lord Chancellor, the judges or any other magistrates, are but the administrators of the powers made by the legislators, i.e. the laws. If any of these judges or magistrates, notwithstanding their real or pretended commission, act contrary to the administration of the Law, they are to be held accountable, culpable, and punishable by Law, according to the nature of their crime.

¶ **179. There is even more reason to believe that the doctrine of absolute passive obedience is a damnable doctrine, because it is inconsistent with the glorious attributes of God, as we know him to be a God of infinite love, mercy, and compassion to all mankind.** He does not choose favourites, for it would make him an unmerciful, cruel, barbarous and tyrannical God, intending mankind to be used as beasts at the will and pleasure of a selected few who are but their equals, until they make them supreme governors.

¶ **180.** Some ignoramuses assert that Adam was an absolute monarch because the father of a family governs by no other law than his own will and pleasure, and a child must obey his father. They claim Adam had an absolute supreme monarchical paternal power and that all kingly authority is in fact fatherly authority and, therefore, irresistible. They further claim that no laws can bind the king or annul his authority.

How could Adam be an absolute monarch, when God gave him the herbs in common with the beasts? (*Genesis* I 29-30) God gave Noah and his sons authority to kill any beast to satisfy their hunger. In *Genesis* IX 5, God says, "*every moving thing that moves, shall be meat for you, even as the herbs have I given you all things*". Cain was cursed for killing Abel and knew that everyone had a right to kill him, by the Law of Nature, for being guilty of blood: "*Every one that found him, should slay him*" (*Genesis* IV 14). God made no exemption to the greatest man living, when found guilty of shedding innocent blood: "*__He that sheds man's blood, by man shall his blood be shed__*".

Neither Noah nor his sons were exempted from this great Law and, therefore, could have no absolute authority. **Since God has nowhere given any man such authority, there can be no such lawful authority. The community cannot make themselves slaves by vesting such an authority in any man. Should they do it, it is not binding, as it is a sin against the Law of Nature, which is the Law of God, which makes all men equal and none slaves.**

¶ **181.** The first fathers of mankind after the Flood did not have royal power. Whatever they had was equally devolved to every one of their sons, as appears by the examples of Noah, Shem, Abraham, Isaac, Jacob, and their children. The first king in Scripture was Nimrod, King of Babylon, the sixth son of Chush, son of Ham, Noah's youngest and cursed son. This was about 130 years after the Flood. Nimrod was chosen by the people, or he could not have been king. Chush, his brother Ham, and his father Noah were then living but were not kings.

¶ **182.** If Noah was heir to Adam, which of Noah's sons was to inherit from him? If by right it descended to all his sons, then all must be entitled, and then it must have descended to all their sons and so on. This means that all men are equal and independent, because all are the offspring of Adam and Noah. If it descended only to the eldest, then there can be only one lawful monarch in the world, and we have no possible way of founding him. This means that the theory of paternal monarchical authority comes to nothing at all.

¶ 183. *"Where people do not allow it, the first born has no right at all above his brethren,"* as the Bishop of Exon acknowledges.

¶ 184. Some ask: *"If a government may be disturbed for any unlawful proceedings of the governor or his ministers, how can any government be safe?"* To this my answer is that it is not lawful for a few persons to oppose their prince if the Law allows them redress. Hence, it is impossible for a few oppressed men to disturb the government much, where the body of the people are not concerned, and the consequences seem not to threaten all. When they do, the people are not quick to disturb the government, as in the time of King Charles II, when the Charters were seized and suppressed to make us slaves. The Laws were perverted to the loss of many innocent lives, dissenters were persecuted for worshipping God according to their consciences, and many other oppressions took place. And yet, the people did not send for a foreign power, nor rise against the government, nor preach sedition, although they were more severely persecuted than the Church was in King James's reign. When the mischief becomes universal and the designs of the rulers notorious, then are the people positioned for righting themselves.

¶ 185. **Anyone who uses force to invade the rights of either prince or people, be it ruler or subject, and lays the foundation for overturning the Constitution and framework of any just government, is guilty of the greatest crime a man is capable of.** That is the crime of shedding blood and causing pillage and desolation, resulting in the breaking up of governments. Anyone who does this is rightfully named an enemy of the nation and pest of mankind.

¶ **186.** In his *History of the Civil Wars*, Clarendon tells us that in the second parliament there was an intention to grant five subsidies, but that meeting was dissolved. The subsidies, however, were instituted throughout the whole kingdom with the same rigour as if an Act had been passed for that purpose. Several gentlemen of various counties were even committed to prison for refusing to pay them.

All these provocations produced no other resentment in the third parliament, than the Petition of Right, which was purchased at five subsidies.

Specific Acts of State were made, and so *Tonnage, Poundage*, and other duties were imposed on merchants, as were particular new and greater impositions laid on trade. The king raised a vast sum of money on the Law of Knighthood, as well as other charges of all kinds, many of which ridiculous, scandalous, and all very grievous. Great fines were instituted on Forest Laws. Every county was ordered to provide an everlasting supply of all sorts. Instead of a ship of war, the Sheriff was to raise money, adding two hundred thousand pounds *per annum* to the king's coffers. All this went on for a few years.

To support these extraordinary ways and to protect their agents, the Council Table and the Star Chamber enlarged their jurisdiction, holding for honourable and just that which pleased and profited.

Proclamations were made to command the people to do what was not enjoined by law and prohibit that which was not prohibited. The offenders were imprisoned and fined with excessive fines, and those foundations of right by which men valued their security were never more in danger of annihilation.

¶ **187.** King Charles I raised money by way of a general loan. If a man was rated in the land subsidy book at 100 in goods, he was to lend one hundred marks; if rated one hundred pounds in land, he was to lend one hundred pounds in money; and so on proportionally for a greater or lesser sum.

Several of St. Clement Danes, the Savoy, the Dutchy, and others within Westminster, who refused to subscribe to the loan, were forced, by Council's Order, to serve in the ships in the king's service. Non-subscribers of high rank in all the counties were made to appear before the Council Table, who committed many of them to prison. Commoners were enlisted as soldiers. For refusing the loan, Sir Peter Hayman was sent to the king's service on the *Palatinate*.

In his two sermons before king and court at Whitehall, Dr. Manwaring defended the heinous doctrine of passive obedience, saying: *The King is not bound to observe the Laws of the Realm concerning the subject's rights and liberties. His royal will and command in imposing loans and taxes without common consent in parliament obliges the subjects' conscience on pain of eternal damnation. Those who refused to pay the loan offended against the supreme authority and are guilty of disloyalty and rebellion.* Also, *the authority of parliament is not necessary for the raising of aids and subsidies.* And further, *the slow proceedings of great assemblies are not fit for emergencies and produce all sorts of obstacles to the just design of princes.*

Archbishop Abbot refused to licence Dr. Sibthorp's sermon (which was the same as Manwaring's) and was sequestered from his office.

The king gave direction for a commission to raise monies by impositions such as an excise to be levied throughout the nation. He ordered the Lord Treasurer to pay thirty thousand pounds to a Dutch merchant for raising one thousand horses, with arms for both cavalry and infantry, which was supposed to enforce the excise.

The horses were ready to come over, but a parliament was called quickly and stopped them.

¶ **188.** The *Vanguard* and seven other English ships were lent to the king of France and employed against La Rochel. The mariners refused the service. The Duke of Buckingham knew about it. The protestants of France implored our king against this involvement, but he expressly commanded the Vice Admiral Pennington to do it.

The commons addressed the public grievances. The king sent a smart letter to the speaker of the House. The commons promised a supply. The king warned that he would not allow his eminent servants to be questioned. He saw that they were taking special aim at the Duke of Buckingham, whom they had charged with many high crimes and misdemeanours.

The Privy Council advised the king to enforce *Tonnage* and *Poundage*. A Commission was issued to deal with recusants. The king required a loan of money and requested London and the port towns to furnish ships for guarding the seas. The deputy lieutenants and the justices of Dorsetshire excused themselves, saying there was no precedent. London was rated at twenty ships but requested an abatement to ten. The council denied it and said that the precedents from history were obedience not direction. Commissions were issued to prevent gatherings and were given martial law powers.

To the imposing of loans was added the billeting of soldiers. Martial law was in place and the soldiers committed great barbarities. Those who refused to lend money to the king were forced to serve in the king's ships; the refusers were either committed or forced to serve as soldiers. The Queen was made to walk to *Tyburn* on penance by her popish priests.

A Commission of excise was granted, and monies disbursed for the raising of German horses.

The Fleet, under the Command of the Earl of Denbeigh, sailed to Rochel. They found that the French ships would not assault them. So after making an appearance only, they returned and left Rochel unrelieved.

Eventually, Manwaring's books were suppressed by proclamation. Although sentenced, Dr. Manwaring was pardoned. Some merchants were committed for not paying *Tonnage* and *Poundage*. When parliament met, they found that **the Petition of Right** was printed with some additions. The originally printed copies were suppressed by order of the King.

The Council's order for levying of *Tonnage* and *Poundage* was read in the House. The speaker was called upon to explain, and he said he didn't dare challenge the king. Warrants of the Council were issued for Hollis and other parliamentarians to appear before them. Hollis, Curriton, Elliot and Valentine showed up but refused to discuss out of parliament anything that was said and done in parliament. They were committed as prisoners in the Tower. A proclamation was published for apprehending others. The Warrants were dated the 5th of March.

The papists in Ireland grew in numbers. Monasteries were there erected, and the papists frequented public meetings and masses as often as the protestants did their churches.

The House of Commons voted:

1. **The charge of ship-money was against the Law, the subject's right and property, and contrary to former resolutions in parliament and to the Petition of Right.**

2. **The extrajudicial opinion of the judges was against the Law.**

3. **The ship-writs were against the Law.**

4. **The judgment against Mr. Hampden about ship-money was against the Law.**

The House of Lords passed the same votes. The next day, **a committee was appointed to draw up a charge of treason against the Lord Keeper Finch and the rest of the judges.**

The king gave a warrant to repair to the lodgings and seal up the trunks, studies, and chambers of certain members of parliament.

The members received a secret notice of this intended action, whereby they got out of the house just before the king came. It was believed that if the king had found them there, he would have called in his guards to seize them. This sudden action was the first visible and apparent signal of all our ensuing miseries.

¶ **189.** Dr. Sacheverell, in his sermon preached at St. Paul's on the 5th of November 1709, to discredit the revolution, falsely asserted that the new King denied the resistance in his declaration. In Sacheverell's view, Parliament set the crown on William's head "on no other title but that of vacancy of the throne."

To undeceive the world, here is the 25th paragraph of the Prince's declaration:

In the last place, we invite and require all persons, all peers of the realm, both Spiritual and Temporal, all lords, lieutenants, deputy lieutenants and all gentlemen, citizens and other commons of all ranks, to come and assist us in the executing of our design against all such who endeavour to oppose us. May we prevent all miseries which would befall the nation if kept under arbitrary government and slavery. May all the violence and disorders, which have overturned the whole Constitution of the English government, be fully redressed in a free and legal parliament.

The falsity of the doctor's other assertion about the vacancy of the throne may be seen by the vote of both Houses of Parliament earlier in this book.

The doctor simply wrests the Scripture to serve his purposes, as do many preachers of the despicable doctrine, insinuating that the Church is in danger, notwithstanding that both Houses of Parliament had voted it out of danger during the life of her majesty.

F I N I S.

ANNEX I

Bill of Rights [1688]

1688 CHAPTER 2 1st Act of William and Mary Session 2

This Act declares the Rights and Liberties of the Subject and settles the succession of the Crown.

<u>X1</u> Whereas on the 13th day of February 1688, the Lords Spiritual and Temporal and the Commons assembled at Westminster, lawfully, fully and freely representing all the estates of the people of this realm. Their Majesties then called and known by the names and style of William and Mary, Prince and Princess of Orange, were present in person when a declaration in writing was made by the said Lords and Commons in the following words:

The Heads of Declaration of Lords and Commons, recited.

Whereas the late King James the Second, by the assistance of various evil councillors, judges and ministers employed by him, endeavoured to subvert and uproot the protestant religion and the Laws and Liberties of this kingdom.

Dispensing and Suspending Power.

By assuming and exercising the power of dispensing with and suspending of Laws, as well as the execution of Laws without the consent of Parliament.

Committing Prelates.

By committing and prosecuting various worthy prelates for humbly petitioning to be excused from concurring to the said assumed power.

Ecclesiastical Commission.

By issuing and causing to be executed a Commission under the Great Seal for erecting a court called The Court of Commissioners for Ecclesiastical Causes.

Levying Money.

By levying money for the use of the Crown by pretence of prerogative for other times and in another manner than was granted by Parliament.

Standing Army.

By raising and keeping a standing army within this Kingdom in time of peace without consent of Parliament and the quartering of soldiers contrary to Law.

Disarming Protestants, &c.

By causing several good protestant subjects to be disarmed at the same time when papists were both armed and employed contrary to Law.

Violating Elections.

By violating the freedom of election of members to serve in Parliament.

Illegal Prosecutions.

By prosecutions in the Court of Kings Bench for matters and causes knowable only in Parliament and by various other arbitrary and illegal actions.

Juries.

And whereas of late years partial corrupt and unqualified persons have been chosen to serve on Juries in trials and particularly diverse Jurors in trials for High Treason which were not freeholders.

Excessive Bail.

And excessive Bail has been required of persons committed in criminal cases to elude the benefit of the Laws made for the Liberty of the Subjects.

Fines.

And excessive fines have been imposed.

Punishments.

And illegal and cruel punishments inflicted.

Grants of Fines, &c. before Conviction, &c.

And several grants and promises made of fines and forfeitures before any conviction or judgement against the persons on whom the same were to be levied. All of which are utterly and directly contrary to the known Laws, Statutes and Freedoms of this realm.

Recital that the late King James II had abdicated the government, and that the throne was vacant, and that the Prince of Orange had written letters to the Lords and Commons for the choosing of representatives in Parliament.

And whereas the said late King James the Second, abdicated the government and left the throne vacant, His [X2 Highnesses] the Prince of Orange (whom it has pleased the Almighty God to make the glorious instrument of delivering this Kingdom from popery and arbitrary power), by the advice of the Lords Spiritual and Temporal and diverse principal persons of the Commons, caused letters to be written to the Lords Spiritual and Temporal, who were protestants, and other letters to the several counties, cities, universities, boroughs and cinque ports for the choosing of such persons to represent them as were of right to be sent to Parliament to meet and sit at Westminster on the 22nd day of January in this year, 1688, in order to institute such an establishment so that their religion, Laws and Liberties might never again be in danger of subvertion, upon which letters elections were made accordingly.

The Subject's Rights.

And thereupon the said Lords Spiritual and Temporal and Commons, pursuant to their respective letters and elections, now assembled fully and freely representing the nation and taking into their most serious consideration the best means for attaining the aforesaid ends, in the first place (as their ancestors in like cases have usually done) for the vindicating and asserting their ancient Rights and Liberties, declare the following:

Dispensing Power.

The pretended power of suspending Laws or the execution of Laws by Regal authority without the consent of Parliament is illegal.

Late dispensing Power.

The pretended power of dispensing with Laws or the execution of Laws by Regal authority as it has been assumed and exercised of late is illegal.

Ecclesiastical Courts illegal.

The Commission for creating the late Court of Commissioners for Ecclesiastical Causes and all other Commissions and Courts of like nature are Illegal and pernicious.

Levying Money.

The levying of money for the use of the Crown by pretence of Prerogative without Grant of Parliament for longer time or in other manner then initially granted is Illegal.

Right to petition.

It is the Right of the Subjects to petition the King and all commitments and prosecutions for such petitioning are Illegal.

Standing Army.

The raising or keeping a standing army within the Kingdom in time of peace, unless with the consent of Parliament, is against the Law.

Subjects' Arms.

The Subjects who are protestants may have arms for their defence suitable to their conditions and as allowed by Law.

Freedom of Election.

That election of Members of Parliament ought to be free.

Freedom of Speech.

The Freedom of Speech and debates or proceedings in Parliament ought not to be impeached or questioned in any court or place out of Parliament.

Excessive Bail.

Excessive bail ought not to be required nor excessive fines imposed nor cruel and unusual punishments inflicted.

Juries.

Jurors ought to be duly impanelled and returned . . . F1

Grants of Forfeitures.

All grants and promises of fines and forfeitures of individual persons before conviction are illegal and void.

Frequent Parliaments.

For redress of all grievances and for the amending, strengthening and preserving of the Laws, Parliaments ought to be held frequently.

The said Rights are claimed. Tender of the Crown. Regal power exercised. Limitation of the Crown.

The People claim, demand and insist, upon all and singular, these premises as their undoubted Rights and Liberties and that no declarations, judgements, actions or proceedings be held to the prejudice of the People in any of the said premisses hereafter ought not in any way to be drawn into consequence or example. To which demand of their Rights, they are particularly encouraged by the declaration of this Highness the Prince of Orange as being the only means for obtaining a full redress and remedy therein.

Having therefore, full confidence that his Highness the Prince of Orange will perfect the deliverance so far advanced by him and will still preserve them from the violation of their Rights, which they have here asserted, and from all other attempts upon their Religion, Rights and Liberties.

The said Lords Spiritual and Temporal and Commons assembled at Westminster resolve that William and Mary, Prince and Princess of Orange, be declared King and Queen of England, France and Ireland and the Dominions thereunto belonging to hold the Crown and Royal Dignity of the said Kingdoms and Dominions to them, the said Prince and Princess, during their lives and the life of their survivor.

And that the sole and full exercise of the Regal Power be only executed by the said Prince of Orange in the names of the said Prince and Princess during their joint lives. After their deceases, the Crown and Royall Dignity of the said Kingdoms and Dominions to be to the heirs of the body of the said Princess. And for default of such issue, to the Princess Anne of Denmark and the heirs of her body. And for default of such issue, to the heirs of the body of the said Prince of Orange. And the Lords Spiritual and Temporal and Commons pray the said Prince and (X3) Princess to accept the same accordingly.

New Oaths of Allegiance, &c.

The Oaths mentioned hereafter ought to be taken by all persons of whom the Oaths of Allegiance and Supremacy might be required by Law instead of them. The old Oaths of Allegiance and Supremacy are abrogated.

Allegiance.

I, A B, do sincerely promise and swear that I will be faithful and bear true allegiance to their Majesties King William and Queen Mary, so help me God.

Supremacy.

I, A B, do swear that I do from my heart abhor, detest and abjure as impious and heretical this damnable doctrine and position that Princes excommunicated or deprived by the Pope or any authority of the See of Rome may be deposed or murdered by their Subjects or any other. And I do declare that no foreign prince, person, prelate, state or potentate has or ought to have any jurisdiction, power, superiority, pre-eminence or authority ecclesiastical or spiritual within this Realm, so help me God.

Acceptance of the Crown. The two Houses to sit. Subjects' Liberties to be allowed, and ministers hereafter to serve according to the same. William and Mary declared King and Queen.

Limitation of the Crown. Papists barred from the Crown. Every King shall make the declaration of 30 Car. II[53]. If under 12 years old, it is to be done after attainment of that age. King's and Queen's Assent.

Upon which their Majesties accepted the Crown and Royall Dignity of the Kingdoms of England, France and Ireland and the Dominions thereunto belonging, according to the resolution and desire of the said Lords and Commons, contained in the above-mentioned Declaration. And thereupon their Majesties were pleased that the said Lords Spiritual and Temporal and Commons, consisting the two Houses of Parliament, should continue to sit and, with their Majesties' Royal concurrence, **make effectual provision for the settlement of the Religion Laws and Liberties of this Kingdom so that in future the same might not be in danger again of being subverted**.

To which the said Lords Spiritual and Temporal and Commons agreed and proceeded to act accordingly. Now in pursuance of the premisses the said Lords Spiritual and Temporal and Commons in Parliament assembled for the ratifying, confirming and establishing the said Declaration and the Articles, Clauses, Matters and Things therein contained by the Force of a Law, made in due form by authority of Parliament, do pray that it may **be declared and enacted that, all and singular, the Rights and Liberties asserted and claimed in the said Declaration are the true ancient and indubitable Rights and Liberties of the People of this Kingdom and so shall be esteemed, allowed, adjudged, deemed and taken to be and that each of the above-mentioned particulars shall be firmly and strictly holden and observed as they are expressed in the said Declaration; And all Officers and Ministers shall serve their Majesties and their successors according to the same in all times to come.**

---

[53] The Act for the more effectual preserving of the king's person and government by disabling papist to sit in either House of Parliament.

The said Lords Spiritual and Temporal and Commons, seriously considering how it has pleased the Almighty God in his marvellous providence and merciful goodness to this nation to provide and preserve their said Majesties' Royal Persons most happily to reign over us on the throne of their ancestors, for which they render to him, from the bottom of their hearts, their humblest thanks and praises. They truly, firmly, assuredly and in the sincerity of their hearts think and hereby recognize, acknowledge and declare that King James the Second having abdicated the government and their Majesties having accepted the Crown and Royall Dignity, [X4 as] previously said, their said Majesties by the Laws of this Realm, became, were, are and by right ought to be our Sovereign Liege Lord and Lady, King and Queene of England, France and Ireland and the Dominions thereunto belonging. To their Princely Persons belong the Royal State Crown and Dignity of the said realms with all honours, styles, titles, regalities, prerogatives, powers, jurisdictions and authorities to the same belonging and appertaining are most fully rightfully and entirely vested, incorporated, united and annexed.

And for preventing of all questions and divisions in this realm by reason of any pretended titles to the Crown and for preserving a certainty in the Succession thereof, in and upon which the unity, peace, tranquillity and safety of this nation under God wholly consist and depend, the said Lords Spiritual and Temporal and Commons beseech their Majesties that it may be enacted, established and declared that the Crown and Regal Government of the said Kingdoms and Dominions, with all and singular the Premisses thereunto belonging and appertaining, shall be and continue to their Majesties and their Survivor during their lives and the life of their survivor. And that the entire perfect and full exercise of the Regal Power and Government be only executed by his Majesty in the names of both their Majesties during their joint lives.

And after their deceases, the said Crown and Premisses shall be and remain to the heirs of the body of her Majesty, and for default of such issue, to her Royall Highness the Princess Anne of Denmark and the heirs of her body; and for default of such issue, to the heirs of the body of his said Majesty.

And thereunto the said Lords Spiritual and Temporal and Commons do, in the name of all the above-mentioned People, most humbly and faithfully submit themselves, their heirs and posterities for ever and faithfully promise that they will stand to maintain and defend their said Majesties and also the limitation and Succession of the Crown herein specified and contained, to the utmost of their powers with their lives and estates against all persons who attempt anything to the contrary. And whereas it has been found by experience that it is inconsistent with the safety and welfare of this protestant Kingdom to be governed by a popish prince F2... the said Lords Spiritual and Temporal and Commons further pray that it may be enacted that each and every person and persons that is, are or shall be reconciled to or shall hold Communion with the See or Church of Rome, or shall profess the popish religion F3... shall be excluded and be for ever incapable to inherit, possess or enjoy the Crown and Government of this Realm and Ireland and the Dominions thereunto belonging or any part of the same or to have use or exercise any Regal Power, Authority or Jurisdiction within the same.

[X5 And in all and every such case or cases, the People of these realms shall be and are hereby absolved of their allegiance]

And the said Crown and Government shall from time to time descend to such person or persons who as protestants should have inherited the same in case the said person or persons so reconciled holding Communion or Professing F4... as previously said were naturally dead.

[X6 And that every King and Queene of this Realm, who at any time hereafter shall succeed to the Imperial Crown of this Kingdom shall, on the first day of the meeting of the first Parliament after his or her coming to the Crown, sitting in his or her throne in the House of Peers in the presence of the Lords and Commons therein assembled, or at his or her Coronation before such person or persons who shall administer the Coronation Oath to him or her at the time of his or her taking the said Oath (which shall first happen), make, subscribe and audibly repeat the Declaration mentioned in the Statute made in the thirtieth year of the reign of King Charles the Second, entitled *An Act for the more Effectual*

Preserving the King's Person and Government by disabling papists from sitting in either House of Parliament.

But if it shall happen that such King or Queene upon his or her Succession to the Crown of this Realm shall be under the age of twelve years, then **every such King or Queen shall make, subscribe and audibly repeat the said Declaration at his or her Coronation** or on the first day of the meeting of the first Parliament as said before, which shall first happen after such King or Queen has attained the said age of twelve years.]

All which their Majesties are contented and pleased shall be declared, enacted and established by authority of this present Parliament and **shall stand, remain and be the Law of this Realm for ever.** And the same are by their said Majesties, by and with the advice and consent of the Lords Spiritual and Temporal and Commons in Parliament assembled, and by the authority of the same declared, enacted and established accordingly.

ANNEX II

Coronation Oath Act 1688

1688 CHAPTER 6 1 William and Mary

An Act for Establishing the Coronation Oath.

Oath heretofore framed in doubtful Words.

Whereas by the Law and ancient usage of this Realm, the Kings and Queens thereof have taken a solemn Oath upon the Evangelists at their respective Coronations to **maintain the Statutes, Laws and Customs of the said Realm and all the People and inhabitants thereof in their Spiritual and Civil Rights and Properties**. But since the Oath itself administered on such occasion was previously framed in **doubtful words and expressions with relation to ancient Laws and Constitutions** currently unknown, therefore, one uniform Oath may be taken in all times to come by the Kings and Queens of this Realm and to them respectively administered at the time of their Coronation.

II Oath hereafter mentioned to be administered by the Archbishop of Canterbury, etc.

May it please Your Majesties that the Oath herein mentioned and hereafter expressed, shall and may be administered to their most Excellent Majesties King William and Queen Mary (whom God long preserve) at the time of their Coronation in the presence of all persons that shall be then and there present at the solemnizing thereof by the Archbishop of Canterbury or the Archbishop of York or either of them or any other Bishop of this Realm, whom the King's Majesty shall thereunto appoint and who shall be respectively authorized to administer the Oath in the following manner:

III Form of Oath and Administration thereof.

The Archbishop or Bishop shall say,

Will You solemnly promise and swear **to govern the People of this Kingdom of England and the Dominions thereto belonging according to the Statutes in Parliament agreed on and the Laws and Customs of the same?**

The King and Queen shall say,

I solemnly Promise so to do.

Archbishop or Bishop,

Will You to Your power **cause Law and Justice in mercy to be executed in all Your judgements?**

King and Queen,

I will.

Archbishop or Bishop.

Will You to the utmost of Your power **maintain the Laws of God,** the true profession of the Gospel and the protestant reformed religion established by Law? And will You Preserve unto the Bishops and Clergy of this Realm and to the Churches committed to their Charge all such Rights and Privileges as by Law do or shall appertain to them or any of them.

King and Queen,

All this I promise to do.

After this the King and Queen laying His and Her Hand upon the Holy Gospels, shall say,

King and Queen

The things which I have here before promised I will perform and keep, so help me God.

Then the King and Queen shall kiss the Book.

IV Oath to be administered to all future Kings and Queens.

And the said Oath shall be in like manner administered to every King or Queen who shall succeed to the Imperial Crowne of this Realm at their respective Coronations by one of the Archbishops or Bishops of this Realm of England as thereunto appointed by such King or Queen respectively and in the presence of all persons that shall be attending, assisting or otherwise present at their respective Coronations, notwithstanding any Law, Statute or Usage to the contrary.

ANNEX III

Act of Settlement 1700

[…]

IV The Laws and Statutes of the Realm confirmed.

And whereas **the Laws of England are the Birthright of the People thereof and all the Kings and Queens who shall ascend the throne of this Realm ought to administer the government of the same according to the said Laws and all their Officers and Ministers ought to serve them respectively according to the same.** The said Lords Spiritual and Temporal and Commons, therefore, further humbly pray **that all the Laws and Statutes of this Realm for securing the established religion and the Rights and Liberties of the People thereof and all other Laws and Statutes of the same now in force may be ratified and confirmed. The same are by His Majesty, by and with the advice and consent of the said Lords Spiritual and Temporal and Commons, and by authority of the same, ratified and confirmed accordingly.**

ANNEX IV

The Coronation Oath of Charles III (6 May 2023)

The Oath

The King places his hand on the Bible, and the Archbishop administers the Oath.

Archbishop of Canterbury: **Will you solemnly promise and swear to govern the Peoples of the United Kingdom of Great Britain and Northern Ireland, your other Realms and the Territories to any of them belonging or pertaining, according to their respective laws and customs?**

The King: I solemnly promise so to do.

Archbishop of Canterbury: Will you to your power cause Law and Justice, in Mercy, to be executed in all your judgements?

The King: I will.

Archbishop of Canterbury: Will you to the utmost of your power maintain the Laws of God and the true profession of the Gospel? Will you to the utmost of your power maintain in the United Kingdom the Protestant Reformed Religion established by law? Will you maintain and preserve inviolably the settlement of the Church of England, and the doctrine, worship, discipline, and government thereof, as by law established in England? And will you preserve unto the Bishops and Clergy of England, and to the Churches there committed to their charge, all such rights and privileges as by law do or shall appertain to them or any of them?

The King: **All this I promise to do**. The things which I have here before promised I will perform and keep. **So help me God**.

Archbishop of Canterbury: Your Majesty, are you willing to make, subscribe and declare to the statutory Accession Declaration Oath?

The King: I am willing.

The King: **I Charles do solemnly and sincerely in the presence of God profess, testify, and declare that I am a faithful Protestant, and that I will, according to the true intent of the enactments which secure the Protestant succession to the Throne, uphold and maintain the said enactments to the best of my powers according to law.**

Printed in Great Britain
by Amazon

47136974R00066